The Spelling Bee Speller

Volume 3

The Final Rounds

The Spelling Bee Speller

Volume 3: The Final Rounds

Sam H. Chang, Ph.D.
with
Frank T. Phipps, Ph.D.

Hondale Inc., *Publishers*
Akron, Ohio

Library of Congress Catalog Card Number: 81-90754
ISBN 0-942462-03-3

Printed in the United States of America

10 9 8 7 6 5 4 3 2

The Spelling Bee Speller is a three-volume set:

Volume 1: THE SPELLING BEE SPELLER, THE FIRST ROUND

Volume 2: THE SPELLING BEE SPELLER, THE MIDDLE ROUNDS

Volume 3: THE SPELLING BEE SPELLER, THE FINAL ROUNDS

You can get Volumes 1, 2, or 3 separately — or all three as a set.

Published by

Hondale, Inc.
553 Auburndale Avenue
Akron, Ohio 44313

To spelling bee coaches, directors, pronouncers, and judges, who make spelling bees possible for the spellers

Cover design by Eric Swanson

Back cover photo by Pete Schwepker, Copyright © 1982,
                    The Arizona Republic, Reprinted
                    with permission

Bee cartoon (page xviii) by Polly Keener

Composition by Oberlin Printing Co.

Contents

Preface To Volume 3:
The Final Rounds

This is the third of a three-volume series *The Spelling Bee Speller*, a self-study guide to spelling practice and vocabulary building. The 1000 key words in this volume are a little harder and more challenging than those in *The First Round* or *The Middle Rounds*.

If you have studied the first two volumes, you can skip the following introductory chapters and go directly to the practice words on page 1. On the other hand, if you haven't studied either of the first two volumes, please read the introductory chapters first. They explain what this book is about and how to use it.

Spelling Bees in These United States, beginning on page 202, is a collection of newspaper articles about spelling bees. These articles describe what spelling bees are like around the country and give hints on how to succeed in them.

Acknowledgments: Many persons contributed to this book. Especially, I thank the following editors and friends: Dr. Frank T. Phipps, Professor Emeritus of English, the University of Akron. For many years Dr. Phipps has served as pronouncer and chief judge of the *Akron Beacon Journal* Spelling Bee; Linda M. Herrington, English teacher and spelling coach, Simon Perkins Middle School, Akron, Ohio; Paul H. Rohmann, Director, the Kent State University Press. I also thank the many spelling bee directors at various newspapers around the country for the information they've graciously given me.

Welcome To *The Spelling Bee Speller*

What this book is about

The *Spelling Bee Speller* is a new, unique self-study guide, a practice spelling book. Each volume contains 1000 words most often used in spelling bees. Clear pronunciations, easy-to-understand definitions, and brief sample sentences are provided for each practice word. This arrangement enables you to pronounce and understand the words before you spell them. You can use the handy SPELLMARK™ included in this book to check your spelling. Practicing this way is like facing a pronouncer at a spelling bee and, at the same time, having a judge check your spelling, too. This will make your practice interesting and challenging. You'll learn more words faster and easier. And it's fun to do.

How this book can help you in spelling bees

Millions of boys and girls across America participate in spelling bees every year. Champions of classroom and school bees may move up to district and regional bees and then to the national finals. Like Little League Baseball and Peewee Football, spelling bees offer wholesome competition, a favorite American pastime.

To succeed in these spelling bees, you need plenty of practice and some luck. More importantly you need someone to help you choose the right words to study, to pronounce words for you to spell, and to answer your questions about the meaning and the use of the words. You're lucky if you have teachers or parents who can help. But often they don't have enough time to work with you. What you need then is a reliable self-study guide, a companion to practice with. *The Spelling Bee Speller* is especially designed as such a guide and companion for you. This is the first book of its kind. No other book comes close to what you find in *The Spelling Bee Speller*.

How this book got started

This book has evolved from experience I had in helping my three children study for spelling bees. Between 1975 and 1980 they participated in *Akron Beacon Journal* spelling bees in Akron, Ohio, and became champions of their school and district bees. While practicing at home for spelling bees, they followed the method of study in this book. They learned the pronunciation, the meaning, and the use of each word as well as the spelling. This way of practicing helped them win the spelling bees and gain a head start in mastering the English language.

How this book is organized

From the thousands of words my children studied, I with their help picked 3000 favorites, then ranked and compiled them in three volumes. As the titles of the volumes suggest, the words become more difficult with each volume. Here are a few sample words:

VOLUME 1: THE FIRST ROUND:

blizzard, aisle, embarrass, bachelor, vacuum, genuine.

VOLUME 2: THE MIDDLE ROUNDS:

chauffeur, stampede, vaccine, toboggan, grimace, accommodate.

VOLUME 3: THE FINAL ROUNDS:

camouflage, ricochet, silhouette, dilemma, ingenious, resuscitate.

Words are often confusing because they are similar to others in pronunciation or spelling: *rein* and *reign*; *colonel* and *kernel*; *banquet* and *bouquet*; *salon* and *saloon*. Other words are similar in meaning: *jetty* and *levee*; *frolic* and *gambol*. Still others are opposite in meaning: *valor* and *cowardice*; *balmy* and *frigid*. You can best learn these words in pairs or groups, and that's the way you'll find them in *The Spelling Bee Speller.*

What you'll gain from this book

As you can see, the words you study in *The Spelling Bee Speller* are those most often asked in spelling bees as well as those most commonly used in everyday English. Knowing them will surely help you succeed not only in spelling bees but also in speaking and writing better English. *The Spelling Bee Speller* offers you the best way to master these words early in your life. And you will enjoy doing it, too.

How To Use *The Spelling Bee Speller*

How to have your own spelling bee at home or at school

A scene in a spelling bee:

Pronouncer: "Sue, your word is (gam′bəl). It means
to leap and skip about playfully; *to frolic*."

Sue: "(gam′bəl). Does it also mean *to take a risk* or *to bet*?"

Pronouncer: "No."

Sue: "Could you please use it in a sentence?"

Pronouncer: "We watched the lambs (gam′bəl) on the grass."

Sue: "g-a-m-b-o-l."

And Sue goes on to the next round. If Sue misses the word, the judge rings a bell, putting Sue out of the match.

That's the way things go in a spelling bee. The pronouncer gives you a word and explains it. After you spell the word, the judges check your spelling. In the same way you can have your own spelling bee at home or at school when you practice spelling in *The Spelling Bee Speller*.

Here is how it works. Let's look at the first practice word on page 2. Read the word (kar′ ə sel′) in pronunciation symbols printed in heavy black type. I suggest you read it aloud. Then try to spell it. If you wish, you may read the definition and the sample sentence to help you understand the word better. When you're ready to check your spelling, look at number *1* in the answer column on page 3. It tells you the correct spelling is *carousel or carrousel.* Then move down the list to the next practice word.

Where to find correct spelling

When you open the book, you'll see six practice words numbered 1 to 6 on your left-hand page and four practice words numbered 7 to 10 on your right-hand page. Each practice word begins with pronunciation, followed by definition and a sample sentence. The correct spellings of the ten practice words are shown in the answer column on the lower right-hand page.

How to use the SPELLMARK™

Use the SPELLMARK™ to cover the answer column. It will keep you from accidentally seeing the correct spelling of practice words. Before you turn a page, put the SPELLMARK™ under your right-hand page. When you line up the bottom of the SPELLMARK™ with the bottom of the next right-hand page, you'll cover all ten words in the next answer column. Now turn the page. When you're ready to check the spelling of your practice word, slide the SPELLMARK™ down just far enough to uncover the spelling of that word.

How the words are pronounced

A word is often misspelled because it's mispronounced. Pronouncing words correctly is one of the basics you'll learn from *The Spelling Bee Speller*. The pronunciation symbols used in this book are easy to follow. Please spend a little time to become familiar with them. You can find a complete pronunciation key printed inside the front cover. A short pronunciation key is printed inside the back cover and also on the SPELLMARK.™ The short key contains those symbols you'll look up most often.

How your dictionary can help you

The Spelling Bee Speller gives you only one or two common definitions for each word you practice. As you know, a word often has many different meanings. Furthermore, a word is sometimes pronounced differently, depending upon the particular meaning it's used for. The word *permit*, for example, is pronounced (pər mit′) as a verb but often pronounced (pər′mit) as a noun. Whenever you want to know more about a word, look it up in your dictionary. If you don't understand the definitions in a dictionary, try others until you do.

Webster's Third New International Dictionary, the official dictionary of the National Spelling Bee, is the most authoritative, but it is very bulky. Other smaller dictionaries are easier to use for quick reference. You might like to look at *Merriam-Webster, Scott Foresman, American Heritage, Macmillan, Random House*, or other reputable dictionaries. The main point is this: Don't pass over a word until you're sure how it's pronounced, what it means, and how it's spelled.

How to practice and review for perfection

Practice these words every day until you've mastered them. Circle words that are difficult for you; then review them in your next round of study. Do this until you can spell every word with confidence. Write down tough ones on index cards and write the pronunciations on the back. Keep them in a box or some other handy place and review them often.

Once or twice a week have someone help you review. Your parents or friends may read words to you from *The Spelling Bee Speller*, then check your spellings. Together you'll have a good time. It's like baseball batting practice. Let the pitcher throw at you some fast and curve balls. At first you might swing and miss. But if you keep at it, you'll bring your batting average up, and you're on your way to winning a championship.

The Final Rounds

1. **(kar′ə sel′)**
   A merry-go-round.
   The (kar′ə sel′) turned round and round,
   carrying children on its wooden ponies.

2. **(bl īth)** or **(bl īth)**
   Cheerful; merry; joyous.
   In the (bl īth) company of her friends, Katie
   forgot all her worries.

3. **(krō kā′)**
   A game played on the lawn with mallets and
   wooden balls.
   Betsy drove the (krō kā′) ball through the
   wicket.

4. **(pri mir′)**
   A prime minister.
   In some countries the head of an elected
   government is called (pri mir′) instead of
   president.

5. **(pri mir′)**
   The first public presentation.
   After three years in the making, the movie had
   its (pri mir′) last week.

6. **(skal′pəl)**
   A small straight knife with a thin, sharp blade used
   in surgery.
   Steve sharpened his (skal′pəl) before dissecting
   the frog.

7. **(bal′ə rē′nə)**
   A female ballet dancer.
   The (bal′ə rē′nə) twirled beautifully on the tips of her toes.

8. **(stam′ə nə)**
   Power to endure fatigue or hardship; strength.
   Winning a marathon requires much (stam′ə nə).

9. **(än′trā)**
   The main course at a dinner.
   The (än′trā) at the banquet was broiled sirloin steak.

10. **(kri shen′dō)** or **(kri sen′dō)**
    A gradual increase in loudness or force; the peak of such an increase.
    The din reached a (kri shen′dō) as the train thundered by.

---

1. carousel or carrousel
2. blithe
3. croquet
4. premier
5. premiere
6. scalpel
7. ballerina
8. stamina
9. entree
10. crescendo

---

1. **(rik′ə shā′)**
   To bounce along a flat surface.
   "I enjoy watching a pebble (rik′ə shā′) across a pond."

2. **(krō shā′)**
   To make a piece of needlework with a single hooked needle.
   She used orange yarn to (krō shā′) a sweater.

3. **(pə tün′yə)** or **(pə tyün′yə)**
   A garden plant with colorful flowers shaped like funnels.
   A pink (pə tün′yə) bloomed in the window box.

4. **(kü)**
   A sudden and brilliant act; a sudden change in the control of government brought about by a small group.
   The army generals led a bloodless (kü) and toppled the civil government.

5. **(küp)**
   A two-door automobile.
   He traded in his old station wagon for a new sport (küp).

6. **(pləm′ət)**
   To fall straight down; plunge.
   The midair collision caused the airplanes to (pləm′ət) to the ground.

7. **(kam′ə fläzh′)**
   A disguise used to blend something with its
   natural surroundings.
   A (kam′ə fläzh′) of colors hides caterpillars
   from unfriendly eyes.

8. **(brag′ərt)**
   A person who brags very much.
   Everyone thought David was only a (brag′ərt)
   when he said he could beat the champion.

9. **(shə rādz′)**
   A game in which a word is acted out silently,
   usually syllable by syllable, until guessed by the
   other players.
   Linda acted out the word *handkerchief* in
   (shə rādz′).

10. **(pan′ə ram′ə)** or **(pan′ə rä′mə)**
    A clear, complete view in every direction over a
    wide area.
    We saw a (pan′ə ram′ə) of hills and valleys as
    we reached the mountaintop.

---

1. **ricochet**
2. **crochet**
3. **petunia**
4. **coup**
5. **coupe**
6. **plummet**
7. **camouflage**
8. **braggart**
9. **charades**
10. **panorama**

---

1. **(bak′gam′ən)**

   A game for two persons played on a special board with 15 pieces whose moves are determined by throws of the dice.

   I needed double sixes to win the (bak′gam′ən) game.

2. **(in jēn′yəs)**

   Clever; inventive; resourceful.

   Using tools in their bicycle shop, the (in jēn′yəs) Wright brothers built a flying machine.

3. **(in′jə nü′ə tē)** or **(in′jə nyü′ə tē)**

   Cleverness; inventiveness; resourcefulness.

   Steve showed great (in′jə nü′ə tē) when he built a mousetrap out of scrap wood.

4. **(in jen′yü əs)**

   Frank and simple; sincere and artless.

   The farmer's (in jen′yü əs) answers dispelled the policeman's suspicions.

5. **(nä ēv′)**

   Simple-minded; artless.

   He was (nä ēv′) enough to believe all people were honest.

6. **(sə fis′tə kā′təd)**

   Complex; refined; characterized by advanced techniques.

   The spaceship is guided by radars, computers, and other (sə fis′tə kā′təd) equipment.

7. (brō shùr′)
A pamphlet.
The summer camp sent me a (brō shùr′)
showing photos of cabins, beaches, and tennis
courts.

8. (flôr′əd) or (flär′əd)
Ruddy; rosy.
His (flôr′əd) complexion makes him look
sunburned.

9. (grip)
A contagious respiratory disease often called flu.
She had a fever and a runny nose from the
(grip).

10. (bə rā′)
A soft, round cap without a brim.
A black (bə rā′) was perched on the artist's
head.

---

1. backgammon
2. ingenious
3. ingenuity
4. ingenuous
5. naive
6. sophisticated
7. brochure
8. florid
9. grippe
10. beret

---

1. (ē′kwə näks′) or (ek′wə näks′)

   The time of the year when the length of day is the same as the length of night.
   After the autumnal (ē′kwə näks′), days become shorter and nights longer.

2. (säl′stəs) or (sōl′stəs)

   Either of the two times in a year when the sun is farthest from the equator.
   Days become longer and nights shorter after the winter (säl′stəs).

3. (hyü man′ə ter′ē ən)

   Of or promoting human welfare.
   Mistreating prisoners of war violates the (hyü man′ə ter′ē ən) rules of the Geneva Convention.

4. (kwä drü′pəl) or (kwäd′rə pəl)

   A number that is four times as great as another.
   Twelve is the (kwä drü′pəl) of three.

5. (dē′zəl) or (dē′səl)

   A kind of engine that burns oil.
   This car has a (dē′zəl) engine instead of a gasoline engine.

6. (pə tēt′)

   Small; dainty.
   His wife, a (pə tēt′) blonde, weighs only ninety pounds.

7. (mer'ē mā'king)
Merry enjoyment; fun.
People go to carnivals for (mer'ē mā'king).

8. (mer'i mənt)
Amusement; laughter and gaiety.
They enjoyed singing, dancing, and other
(mer'i mənt) at the party.

9. (hī'kü)
A short poem of three lines, having five syllables
in the first, seven in the second, and five in the
third.
Jack composed a (hī'kü) and recited it in class.

10. (thi sôr'əs)
A book of synonyms and antonyms.
I looked in a (thi sôr'əs) to find synonyms for
the word *run*.

---

1. equinox
2. solstice
3. humanitarian
4. quadruple
5. diesel
6. petite
7. merrymaking
8. merriment
9. haiku
10. thesaurus

---

1. **(də lem′ə)**
   A situation requiring a difficult choice.
   I was in a (də lem′ə) trying to decide whether to go to the party or stay home and do my homework.

2. **(kwän′dər ē) or (kwän′drē)**
   A state of being uncertain or perplexed.
   Lisa was in a (kwän′dər ē) at the spelling bee when she was asked to spell a word she had never heard before.

3. **(flō til′ə)**
   A fleet of small ships.
   A (flō til′ə) of fishing boats set sail from the port.

4. **(sə fär′ē)**
   A long hunting trip.
   They killed a lion during their African (sə fär′ē).

5. **(in säm′nē ə)**
   Inability to fall asleep.
   Her (in säm′nē ə) is so bad that she can't go to sleep without taking sleeping pills.

6. **(mär′mə lād′)**
   A jam made of the pulp and the rind of fruits.
   I like orange (mär′mə lād′) on my toast.

7. (ek′strə kāt′)
To free from danger or difficulty.
The fox couldn't (ek′strə kāt′) itself from the trap.

8. (är kā′ik)
Out of date; old-fashioned.
The words *thee* and *thou* are (är kā′ik); they are rarely used in today's writing or speech.

9. (är′kīvz′)
A place where public records and historical documents are stored.
The general's letters written during the Civil War are kept in the (är′kīvz′) of the museum.

10. (är′kē äl′ə jəst)
A scientist who studies ancient peoples and cultures through their remains.
The (är′kē äl′ə jəst) spent many years excavating the ancient ruins of Egypt.

---

1. dilemma
2. quandary
3. flotilla
4. safari
5. insomnia
6. marmalade
7. extricate
8. archaic
9. archives
10. archaeologist or archeologist

---

1. **(an'ti rüm)** or **(an'ti rüm)**
   A waiting room at the entrance of another room or
   office.
   The ladies chatted in the (an'ti rüm) while they
   waited to see the doctor.

2. **(an'tə sēd'ənt)**
   Something that comes before another in a series of
   events or developments.
   The attack on Pearl Harbor was an
   (an'tə sēd'ənt) to America's entry into
   World War II.

3. **(an'tə sep'tik)**
   A substance that kills germs and prevents infection.
   Iodine is an effective (an'tə sep'tik).

4. **(an'ti dōt')**
   A medicine that works against a poison; a cure.
   When he was bitten by a snake, doctors saved
   his life with an (an'ti dōt').

5. **(päs'ē)**
   A group of men gathered by a sheriff to help him
   carry out the law.
   The sheriff and his (päs'ē) of twelve men chased
   the fleeing bandits.

6. **(lek'sə kän')** or **(lek'sə kən)**
   A dictionary.
   He can read the Greek New Testament with the
   help of a (lek'sə kän').

7. **(jī rā′shən)**
   The act of turning around; a circular motion; rotation.
   The spinning top made one last (jī rā′shən) before it fell.

8. **(pə rüz′)**
   To read carefully.
   "Please (pə rüz′) your contract before you sign it."

9. **(tô ren′shəl) or (tə ren′shəl)**
   Violent and rapid like a rushing stream of water.
   (tô ren′shəl) rains flooded the streets and the sidewalks.

10. **(kap′səl)**
    A small container holding a dose of medicine that can be swallowed.
    The doctor told him to take one (kap′səl) before every meal.

---

1. **anteroom**
2. **antecedent**
3. **antiseptic**
4. **antidote**
5. **posse**
6. **lexicon**
7. **gyration**
8. **peruse**
9. **torrential**
10. **capsule**

---

1. **(ri küp′)**
   To regain; to make up for.
   Investors (ri küp′) their losses when stock prices rise.

2. **(ri kü′pə rāt′)** or **(ri kyü′pə rāt′)**
   To regain health or strength; to recover.
   She has to stay home a few more days to (ri kü′pə rāt′) from pneumonia.

3. **(kän′və les′)**
   To get better after illness; to recover health.
   After leaving the hospital, he went to Florida to rest and (kän′və les′).

4. **(kō′ə les′)**
   To grow or unite into one.
   The doctor put a cast on Larry's arm to help the broken bone (kō′ə les′).

5. **(rem′ə nis′)**
   To think or talk about things from the past.
   The old friends got together to (rem′ə nis′) about their school days.

6. **(rem′ə nis′ənt)**
   Recalling past happenings; awakening memories.
   Her story was (rem′ə nis′ənt) of an experience I had in school.

7. **(fyôrd)**
   A long, narrow arm of the sea between high cliffs.
   That (fyôrd) is wide and deep enough for a large steamship to sail through.

8. **(kē)**
   A landing place for ships.
   The fishermen unloaded their fish onto the concrete pavement of the (kē).

9. **(di fyü′zhən)**
   The act of spreading widely.
   Books and newspapers contribute to the (di fyü′zhən) of knowledge.

10. **(hā′dā′)**
    The period of greatest strength, popularity, or prosperity.
    In the (hā′dā′) of his powers, Napoleon ruled most of Europe.

---

1. **recoup**
2. **recuperate**
3. **convalesce**
4. **coalesce**
5. **reminisce**
6. **reminiscent**
7. **fjord** or **fiord**
8. **quay**
9. **diffusion**
10. **heyday**

1. **(ek sen′trik)** or **(ik sen′trik)**
   Odd; queer; peculiar.
   That (ek sen′trik) old man carries an umbrella wherever he goes.

2. **(ə näm′ə ləs)**
   Abnormal; deviating from what is common.
   It's (ə näm′ə ləs) for a bird to swim rather than to fly.

3. **(ə näm′ə lē)**
   Something that is abnormal or deviates from what is common.
   A canary that cannot sing is an (ə näm′ə lē).

4. **(kər′ənt)**
   A small seedless berry used for making jelly and jam.
   (kər′ənt) jelly has a delightful flavor and a beautiful red color.

5. **(se tē′)**
   A small sofa; a bench with a back.
   The (se tē′) in that room could seat only two people.

6. **(gü′rü)** or **(gü rü′)**
   A spiritual teacher in the Hindu religion.
   The (gü′rü) taught his followers how to live in peace.

7. **(mas′kə rād′)**
   A party at which people wear masks and
   costumes.
   Mary was dressed like a witch for the
   Halloween (mas′kə rād′).

8. **(dī′ə səs)** or **(dī′ə sēs′)**
   A church district under the authority of a bishop.
   The bishop called a meeting of all priests in his
   (dī′ə səs).

9. **(süd′ə nim)**
   A made-up name used by a writer or an
   entertainer instead of his or her real name; a pen
   name.
   Samuel Clemens wrote his books under the
   (süd′ə nim) Mark Twain.

10. **(shap′ə rōn′)**
    An adult who attends and oversees a social
    gathering of young people.
    The English teacher came to the school dance as
    a (shap′ə rōn′).

---

1. **eccentric**
2. **anomalous**
3. **anomaly**
4. **currant**
5. **settee**
6. **guru**
7. **masquerade**
8. **diocese**
9. **pseudonym**
10. **chaperon** or **chaperone**

---

1. **(lā)** or **(lā′ē)**
   A Hawaiian garland of flowers worn around the neck.
   The Hawaiian dancer wore a (lā) of yellow flowers.

2. **(hə lü′sə nā′shən)**
   An experience of seeing or hearing things that are not real.
   The ghost he saw was only a (hə lü′sə nā′shən) caused by his high fever.

3. **(sō′jərn)** or **(sō jərn′)**
   A temporary stay.
   He returned home after a summer's (sō′jərn) in Europe.

4. **(krə vat′)**
   A necktie; a scarf worn as a necktie.
   He wore a wide red (krə vat′) that covered the front of his shirt.

5. **(en kəm′pəs)** or **(in kəm′pəs)**
   To form a circle around; to include.
   He is writing a history book that will (en kəm′pəs) all the major events of the Civil War.

6. **(in sin′ə rā′tər)**
   A furnace for burning waste.
   We burn our trash in an (in sin′ə rā′tər).

7. (är′sə nəl)
A building where guns and ammunition are made and stored.
This (är′sə nəl) produced cannon balls for the Confederate Army.

8. (är′mər ē)
A place where weapons are made or stored; a building with drill halls used for training a military reserve force.
The army reserve unit met for drills at the (är′mər ē).

9. (krī tir′ē ən)
A standard of judgment; a test.
Profit is an important (krī tir′ē ən) of business success.

10. (pēk)
Anger caused by wounded pride.
Jenny left the meeting in a (pēk) because everyone ignored her suggestion.

---

1. lei
2. hallucination
3. sojourn
4. cravat
5. encompass
6. incinerator
7. arsenal
8. armory
9. criterion
10. pique

---

1. **(mə näp′ə lē)**
   The sole control over making or selling a product or service.
   The telephone company has a (mə näp′ə lē) in our city.

2. **(mə nät′n əs)**
   Tiring because of sameness; dull; not changing.
   The speaker's (mə nät′n əs) voice made some people fall asleep in their chairs.

3. **(män′ə lôg′)** or **(män′ə läg′)**
   A speech by one person in the company of others.
   No one asked any questions while the professor rambled on with his (män′ə lôg′).

4. **(män′ə kəl)** or **(män′i kəl)**
   An eyeglass for one eye.
   The man had a gold-rimmed (män′ə kəl) for his left eye.

5. **(bär′nə kəl)** or **(bär′ni kəl)**
   A small shell-covered sea animal that attaches itself to the bottoms of ships or underwater rocks.
   A (bär′nə kəl) clings to the hull of a ship.

6. **(twē′zərz)**
   Small pincers used for grasping or pulling.
   She pulled the splinter out of my finger with (twē′zərz).

7. **(jam′bə rē′)**
   A noisy merrymaking or festival.
   The city celebrated its bicentennial with a (jam′bə rē′) featuring concerts, parades, and fireworks.

8. **(i nən′sē ā′shən)**
   The way of pronouncing words and syllables.
   One must have clear (i nən′sē ā′shən) to become a radio announcer.

9. **(kri tēk′)**
   A critical review or commentary.
   The English teacher wrote a one-page (kri tēk′), suggesting ways to improve John's composition.

10. **(mas′ə kər)**
    A brutal killing of a large number of people or animals.
    None of Custer's troops survived the Indian (mas′ə kər) at Little Bighorn.

---

1. monopoly
2. monotonous
3. monologue
4. monocle
5. barnacle
6. tweezers
7. jamboree
8. enunciation
9. critique
10. massacre

The Final Rounds

1. **(si sēd′)**
   To withdraw from an organization.
   Because of the dispute, the Southern states
   decided to (si sēd′) from the Union.

2. **(si sesh′ən)**
   The act of withdrawing from an organization.
   The Southern states formed a separate,
   independent nation after their (si sesh′ən) from
   the Union.

3. **(se sā′shən)**
   A ceasing; a halt.
   The United Nations called for a (se sā′shən) of
   fighting between the two countries.

4. **(pôr′sə lən)** or **(pôrs′lən)**
   A white, glasslike earthenware.
   "Be careful with this (pôr′sə lən) vase because it
   will break easily."

5. **(pər′ mē āt′)**
   To spread or pass through.
   Water can (pər′mē āt′) cotton and sand.

6. **(kī ō′tē)**
   A small wolflike animal of western North America.
   The (kī ō′tē) came out at night to prey on the
   farmer's sheep.

---

7. (präd'ə jē)
A highly talented person.
Mozart, a child (präd'ə jē), composed music at
the age of five.

8. (i nam'əl)
A smooth, hard coating used for protection or
decoration.
This cooking pot is made of steel coated with
white (i nam'əl).

9. (säm brar'ō) or (säm brer'ō)
A large broad-brimmed hat worn in Mexico and
the southwestern United States.
The (säm brar'ō) shaded the cowboy's face from
the scorching sun.

10. (pē'dē ə trish'ən)
A medical doctor who specializes in the care of
babies and children.
When the baby had a fever, Mother took him
to a (pē'dē ə trish'ən).

---

1. secede
2. secession
3. cessation
4. porcelain
5. permeate
6. coyote
7. prodigy
8. enamel
9. sombrero
10. pediatrician

---

1. **(ri tal′ē āt′)**
    To act in return; to get even.
    Our army will (ri tal′ē āt′) if we're attacked.

2. **(mas′təf)**
    A large, strong dog with a heavy head and a
    smooth coat.
    "My neighbor keeps a (mas′təf) as a watchdog."

3. **(sem′ə när′)**
    A meeting held for exchange of information and
    discussion.
    The famous scientist gave a lecture at the
    (sem′ə när′).

4. **(sem′ə ner′ē)**
    A school for the training of ministers and priests.
    He became a priest after graduating from the
    (sem′ə ner′ē).

5. **(in dīt′)**
    To make a formal accusation of a crime.
    The grand jury had enough evidence to (in dīt′)
    him for robbery.

6. **(pyü′tər)**
    A metal of silver-gray color made by combining tin,
    copper, and other metals.
    This mug is very heavy, because it's made of
    (pyü′tər).

7. **(dis kôrd′ənt)**
Not in harmony; harsh.
Quacking in a (dis kôrd′ənt) chorus, the
frightened ducks waddled away.

8. **(dis′ə nənt)**
Lacking harmony; harsh in sound.
You'll make (dis′ə nənt) sounds if you hit
wrong keys on the piano.

9. **(yü tō′pē ə)**
An ideal place or life.
His idea of a (yü tō′pē ə) is to spend the
winter in Florida and the summer in Maine.

10. **(shə grin′)**
A feeling of annoyance caused by disappointment,
failure, or embarrassment.
The quarterback threw a long pass, but to his
(shə grin′) it was intercepted.

---

1. retaliate
2. mastiff
3. seminar
4. seminary
5. indict
6. pewter
7. discordant
8. dissonant
9. utopia
10. chagrin

---

1. **(mat′ə dôr′)**
   The chief bullfighter who is supposed to kill the bull.
   The (mat′ə dôr′) thrust his sword at the bull.

2. **(pər′jər ē)**
   The act of testifying falsely under oath.
   If a witness tells a lie in court, he can be charged with (pər′jər ē).

3. **(in sip′ē ənt)**
   Just beginning; in an early stage.
   She has an (in sip′ē ənt) cold and needs plenty of liquids and rest.

4. **(ə lüd′)**
   To refer indirectly; to hint at.
   "Don't mention or even (ə lüd′) to it when you see him."

5. **(kət′lər ē)**
   Knives, forks, and spoons for table use.
   She bought a set of (kət′lər ē) including a carving knife.

6. **(val′əns)**
   A short drapery hanging across the top of a window.
   She hung new curtains and a matching (val′əns) in the kitchen window.

7. **(kan'ə nād')**

A heavy, continuous firing of artillery. The (kan'ə nād') rained shells upon the enemy fortress.

8. **(käl'ə nād')**

A row of columns set at regular intervals. A (käl'ə nād') of ten white pillars adorns the front of the museum.

9. **(em'ər əld) or (em'rəld)**

Bright-green. The yacht glided over the (em'ər əld) sea.

10. **(päl'ē glät')**

A person who speaks several languages. Our tour guide was a (päl'ē glät') who spoke German, French, and Spanish fluently.

---

1. **matador**
2. **perjury**
3. **incipient**
4. **allude**
5. **cutlery**
6. **valance**
7. **cannonade**
8. **colonnade**
9. **emerald**
10. **polyglot**

---

1. (in′käg nē′tō) or (in käg′nə tō)
   In disguise; with one's identity concealed.
   Dressed like a monk, the king came
   (in′käg nē′tō) to visit the poor peasants.

2. (plan′ə tar′ē əm) or (plan′ə ter′ē əm)
   A room or a building with a domed ceiling for
   showing the movements of heavenly bodies.
   "I learned a lot about stars during my visit to
   the (plan′ə tar′ē əm)."

3. (sep′tər)
   A staff held by a king as a symbol of authority.
   Holding a golden (sep′tər), the king sat on the
   throne when he received the ambassador.

4. (bə kē′nē)
   A woman's brief two-piece bathing suit.
   Amy wore a (bə kē′nē) when she went
   swimming.

5. (klôr′ēn′) or (klôr′ən)
   A chemical, often used to purify water.
   The water in the swimming pool has so much
   (klôr′ēn′) that it hurts my eyes.

6. (skaf′əld)
   A platform used to support builders, painters, or
   others when working on a tall building.
   They stood on a (skaf′əld) to wash the windows
   of that tall building.

7. **(i lis′ət)**
   To draw out.
   Detectives questioned witnesses to (i lis′ət) information about the robbery suspect.

8. **(i lis′ət)**
   Unlawful; improper; not allowed.
   A man was arrested for the (i lis′ət) sale of drugs.

9. **(lə jit′ə mət)**
   Reasonable; justifiable; lawful.
   As Tom had no (lə jit′ə mət) excuse for not going to school, he pretended he was sick.

10. **(tram′pə lēn′)** or **(tram′pə lēn′)**
    A strong canvas or net used in acrobatic exercises.
    Gary practiced tumbling on the (tram′pə lēn′).

---

1. **incognito**
2. **planetarium**
3. **scepter**
4. **bikini**
5. **chlorine**
6. **scaffold**
7. **elicit**
8. **illicit**
9. **legitimate**
10. **trampoline**

---

1. **(per'ə skōp')**
   An instrument made with a tube and mirrors
   allowing a person to see things indirectly.
   The captain peered into the (per'ə skōp') of the
   submarine to look for enemy ships.

2. **(pə rim'ə tər)**
   The outer boundary of an area.
   A barbed-wire fence marked the (pə rim'ə tər) of
   the army camp.

3. **(kō'pē əs)**
   Plentiful; abundant.
   "We ate a (kō'pē əs) amount of hot dogs and
   potato chips at the picnic."

4. **(vər'sə təl)**
   Able to do many things well.
   Norma is a (vər'sə təl) athlete; she excels at
   tennis, basketball, and hockey.

5. **(ōr'ē ōl')** or **(ôr'ē ōl')**
   A songbird with black-and-orange or black-and-
   yellow feathers.
   An (ōr'ē ōl') built a hanging nest in the tree.

6. **(säd'ər)** or **(sôd'ər)**
   A metal used when melted for joining or mending
   other metal surfaces.
   Jim used (säd'ər) to join the copper wires.

7. **(nīt′n gāl′)** or **(nī′ting gāl′)**

A small yellowish-brown songbird of Europe. Many poets have written about the sweet song of the (nīt′n gāl′).

8. **(mäl′ə kyül)**

The smallest particle of a substance still displaying the properties of that substance.

A water (mäl′ə kyül) is made of one oxygen atom and two hydrogen atoms.

9. **(ôr′ə)**

A distinctive quality or air surrounding a person. He had an (ôr′ə) of mystery about him because he always looked as if he were in deep thought.

10. **(min′ē ə chər)** or **(min′ə chər)**

Very small.

Carol's (min′ē ə chər) doll house is smaller than that portable television set.

---

1. periscope
2. perimeter
3. copious
4. versatile
5. oriole
6. solder
7. nightingale
8. molecule
9. aura
10. miniature

---

1. **(sə brī′ə tē)** or **(sō brī′ə tē)**
   The state of being sober, modest, or serious.
   When Rip Van Winkle regained (sə brī′ə tē), he found himself an old man.

2. **(tem′pər əns)** or **(tem′prəns)**
   The complete avoidance of alcoholic drinks.
   Dan's grandmother never served beer in her house because she believed in (tem′pər əns).

3. **(ab′stə nəns)**
   The practice of self-restraining, as in eating and drinking.
   The monks took a vow of (ab′stə nəns) from alcohol and tobacco.

4. **(dis′ər tā′shən)**
   A formal essay.
   Writing a (dis′ər tā′shən) was a requirement for his doctoral degree.

5. **(slē′zē)**
   Of poor quality; cheap.
   Her new dress, made of a (slē′zē) rayon fabric, tore at the seams.

6. **(am nē′zhə)**
   Loss of memory.
   He suffered from (am nē′zhə) and couldn't remember his own name.

7. **(wind′ləs)**
A lifting or hoisting machine consisting of a drum wound with rope or cable and turned by a crank.
He turned the (wind′ləs) to draw a bucket of water from the well.

8. **(kak′ē) or (kä′kē)**
A yellowish brown color; a cotton or wool cloth of this color.
The soldiers were dressed in neat (kak′ē) uniforms.

9. **(plat′nəm) or (plat′n əm)**
A silver-white precious metal.
(plat′nəm) looks like silver but is more costly.

10. **(kat′ə pəlt′)**
An ancient weapon for hurling rocks, spears, or arrows.
A slingshot is a miniature (kat′ə pəlt′).

---

1. sobriety
2. temperance
3. abstinence
4. dissertation
5. sleazy
6. amnesia
7. windlass
8. khaki
9. platinum
10. catapult

---

1. (mem'wärz) or (mem'wôrz)
   An autobiography.
   The general wrote his (mem'wärz) telling of the
   wars he had fought in.

2. (gü'bər nə tôr'ē əl)
   Of a governor.
   The governor won the (gü'bər nə tôr'ē əl)
   election for a second term.

3. (grə tü'ə tē) or (grə tyü'ə tē)
   A tip.
   The restaurant added a (grə tü'ə tē) of fifteen
   percent to the price of our dinners.

4. (grat'əs) or (grā'təs)
   Free; without charge.
   The concert tickets were sent (grat'əs) to the
   Glee Club members.

5. (ə fil'ē āt')
   To join or associate with.
   The club members voted to (ə fil'ē āt')
   themselves with their national organization.

6. (kəv'ə nənt)
   A solemn agreement.
   Couples enter a (kəv'ə nənt) of lifetime
   partnership when they marry.

7. **(shə lak′)**
A kind of thin, clear varnish.
He put a coat of (shə lak′) on the table to give it a smooth, shiny finish.

8. **(man′ə fest′)**
To show plainly; to reveal.
After suffering a head injury, the man began to (man′ə fest′) strange behavior.

9. **(par′ə däks′)**
A statement that seems to disagree with itself but is perhaps true.
The saying "The hurrier I go, the behinder I get" is a (par′ə däks′).

10. **(ôr′kəd)**
A beautiful tropical flower having three petals.
She wore a white (ôr′kəd) pinned to the lapel of her coat.

---

1. **memoirs**
2. **gubernatorial**
3. **gratuity**
4. **gratis**
5. **affiliate**
6. **covenant**
7. **shellac**
8. **manifest**
9. **paradox**
10. **orchid**

---

1. **(kwôr'ən tēn')** or **(kwär'ən tēn')**
   The act of keeping someone away from others to prevent spreading disease.
   The crew of the ship was placed under (kwôr'ən tēn') when smallpox was discovered among them.

2. **(man'ə fōld')**
   Of many kinds; various.
   That teacher has (man'ə fōld') duties; besides teaching classes, he supervises the science lab, coaches the wrestling team, and directs the band.

3. **(prāt)**
   To talk idly and foolishly.
   If you let him, he will (prāt) for hours about his fishing trips.

4. **(häm'ə nē)**
   Kernels of white corn, often hulled and coarsely ground.
   My aunt in Georgia cooks (häm'ə nē) grits every morning for breakfast.

5. **(mə trik'yə lā'shən)**
   Enrollment in a college or a university.
   (mə trik'yə lā'shən) for entering freshmen will begin on Wednesday.

6. **(ôr'ə kəl)** or **(är'ə kəl)**
   A person in ancient Greece who delivered a god's messages to visitors at his shrine.
   The ancient Greeks believed in the prophecies of the (ôr'ə kəl).

7. **(kə nən′drəm)**
   A riddle whose answer is a pun; a puzzling problem.
   "What has three feet and cannot run?" The answer to this (kə nən′drəm) is *a yardstick.*

8. **(i nig′mə)**
   A puzzle; a person who is not easily understood.
   The child was an (i nig′mə); not even his parents knew what he was really up to.

9. **(tam′bə rēn′)**
   A small drum with metal disks around the rim, carried and shaken with one hand, struck with the other.
   She jingled the (tam′bə rēn′) as she danced.

10. **(kôr säzh′)**
   A small bouquet worn on a woman's dress.
   She came to the dance wearing a (kôr säzh′) of white orchids on her blue dress.

---

1. **quarantine**
2. **manifold**
3. **prate**
4. **hominy**
5. **matriculation**
6. **oracle**
7. **conundrum**
8. **enigma**
9. **tambourine**
10. **corsage**

---

1. **(mō tēf′)**
   A pattern; a theme.
   Our kitchen curtains have a tulip (mō tēf′).

2. **(zin′ē ə)**
   A garden plant with bright flowers of many colors.
   (Zin′ē ə) flowers bloom in many colors.

3. **(nik′ə tēn′)**
   A poison found in tobacco.
   Because he smoked heavily, his teeth were yellow
   from (nik′ə tēn′) stains.

4. **(wŭs′təd) or (wər′stəd)**
   A fabric made of firmly twisted woolen yarn.
   Jack wore a brown (wŭs′təd) jacket over his
   green sweater.

5. **(mar′ə gōld′)**
   A garden plant with bright flowers of many colors.
   The yellow and orange (mar′ə gōld′) flowers
   bloomed all summer.

6. **(sə rôr′ə tē) or (sə rär′ə tē)**
   A club of women students at college.
   She preferred living in the (sə rôr′ə tē) house to
   living in the dormitory.

7. **(kə pich′ə lāt′)**
   To surrender; to give in.
   When their food and ammunition ran out, the
   defending army had no choice but to
   (kə pich′ə lāt′).

8. **(sə kəm′)**
   To yield; to give in.
   She tends to (sə kəm′) to her appetite and
   forget about her diet.

9. **(trel′əs)**
   A framework of wood or metal used to support
   climbing plants.
   Blooming red roses covered the white (trel′əs).

10. **(kris′ən)**
    To give a name to.
    The queen attended the ceremony to (kris′ən)
    the ship.

---

1. **motif**
2. **zinnia**
3. **nicotine**
4. **worsted**
5. **marigold**
6. **sorority**
7. **capitulate**
8. **succumb**
9. **trellis**
10. **christen**

---

1. (sī käl'ə jəst)
   A scientist who specializes in the study of the mind.
   The (sī käl'ə jəst) gave the boy an examination
   to see why he was a slow learner in school.

2. (sə kī'ə trəst) or (sī kī'ə trəst)
   A medical doctor who specializes in the treatment
   of mental disorders.
   Dr. Wilson is a (sə kī'ə trəst) at the mental
   hospital.

3. (dis'ə pāt')
   To make disappear.
   Her kind words helped (dis'ə pāt') his anger.

4. (mə ras')
   A tract of soft, swampy ground; a marsh; a bog.
   The heavy rain turned the field into a (mə ras')
   of mud.

5. (kwag'mīr') or (kwäg'mīr')
   A soft, muddy ground that gives way under the
   foot.
   The jeep was stuck in a (kwag'mīr') near the
   creek.

6. (bī'ü) or (bī'ō)
   A sluggish, marshy section of a lake or a river.
   Many wading birds live along the shores of that
   (bī'ü).

7. **(dis trôt')**
Very worried; anxious.
The (dis trôt') parents searched the woods for their lost child.

8. **(jü dish'ē er'ē)** or **(jü dish'ər ē)**
Having to do with the courts of justice.
The Supreme Court is the highest (jü dish'ē er'ē) authority in the United States.

9. **(pyü'jə ləst)**
A professional boxer.
The (pyü'jə ləst) knocked his opponent out in the second round of the match.

10. **(sham pān')**
A sparkling wine.
The queen christened the ship by breaking a bottle of (sham pān') on its hull.

---

1. **psychologist**
2. **psychiatrist**
3. **dissipate**
4. **morass**
5. **quagmire**
6. **bayou**
7. **distraught**
8. **judiciary**
9. **pugilist**
10. **champagne**

---

1. **(kär niv′ər əs)**
   Feeding on flesh.
   (kär niv′ər əs) animals like lions and tigers use their sharp claws and teeth to catch prey.

2. **(hər biv′ər əs)**
   Feeding on plants.
   Deer and sheep are (hər biv′ər əs) animals.

3. **(äm niv′ər əs)**
   Eating both plant and animal food.
   Raccoons and mice are (äm niv′ər əs) animals that eat everything from grain to fish.

4. **(äm nip′ə tənt)**
   Having the power to do all things.
   Aladdin was (äm nip′ə tənt) as long as he had the magic lamp.

5. **(äm nish′ənt)**
   Knowing and understanding all things.
   The writer of the novel seemed (äm nish′ənt) because he knew everything happening to the characters in his book.

6. **(ə kü′stiks)**
   The qualities of a room that determine how well sound is heard in it.
   This auditorium has fine (ə kü′stiks); you can hear as well in the back as in the front.

7. **(dou′ə jər)**
A wealthy elderly woman.
The (dou′ə jər) willed her mansion to an orphanage.

8. **(hal′ə bət)**
A large ocean fish with a flat body.
The fisherman caught a (hal′ə bət) weighing more than five hundred pounds.

9. **(chôr′tl)**
A chuckle; a gleeful snorting sound.
Jack let out a merry (chôr′tl) while reading the comics.

10. **(sē er′ə)**
A rugged range of mountains.
The snowcapped peaks of the (sē er′ə) could be seen in the distance.

---

1. **carnivorous**
2. **herbivorous**
3. **omnivorous**
4. **omnipotent**
5. **omniscient**
6. **acoustics**
7. **dowager**
8. **halibut**
9. **chortle**
10. **sierra**

---

1. **(äb′ə lisk)**
   A four-sided column tapering at the top like a pyramid.
   The Washington Monument is an (äb′ə lisk) 555 feet tall.

2. **(vag′ə bänd′)**
   A person wandering idly from place to place without a home.
   The student spent the summer as a (vag′ə bänd′) hitchhiking around the country.

3. **(kän′ə tā′shən)**
   A suggested or implied meaning.
   The word *spring* has a (kän′ə tā′shən) of hope and life.

4. **(tü məl′chù əs)** or **(tyü məl′chü əs)**
   Noisy; excited.
   The crowd gave their hero a (tü məl′chù əs) welcome.

5. **(lit′ə gā′shən)**
   The act of carrying on a lawsuit.
   To avoid a lengthy (lit′ə gā′shən), they settled their dispute out of court.

6. **(pôr′ij)** or **(pär′ij)**
   A soft food made of ground grain or cereal boiled in water or milk.
   Oatmeal is a (pôr′ij) often served with milk at breakfast.

7. (dī′vərz)
Various; several.
"I can give you (dī′vərz) reasons why you shouldn't smoke."

8. (dī vərs′), (də vərs′), or (dī′vərs)
Different; unlike.
The circus trucks hauled cargo as (dī vərs′) as elephants, tents, and kitchen equipment.

9. (ə test′)
To testify; to give proof of.
These certificates (ə test′) to the doctor's ability to practice medicine.

10. (in′tər əm)
An interval of time between two events; the meantime.
In the (in′tər əm), the sheriff was the acting mayor.

---

1. obelisk
2. vagabond
3. connotation
4. tumultuous
5. litigation
6. porridge
7. divers
8. diverse
9. attest
10. interim

---

1. **(pri lim′ə ner′ē)**
   Coming before or preparing for a main event.
   Nominating a candidate is a (pri lim′ə ner′ē)
   step in an election.

2. **(tər′koiz) or (tər′kwoiz)**
   Blue-green.
   (tər′koiz) waters surround the white beaches of
   the tropical isle.

3. **(skrüt′n ē)**
   A careful observation, inquiry, or inspection.
   Candidates for government offices undergo public
   (skrüt′n ē) during their election campaigns.

4. **(in′sər moun′tə bəl)**
   Incapable of being overcome.
   These problems won't be (in′sər moun′tə bəl) if
   you work hard at them.

5. **(tər′mə näl′ə jē)**
   The special words used in a field of study, as in
   science or business.
   We couldn't understand the medical
   (tər′mə näl′ə jē) in the doctor's speech.

6. **(di tir′ē ə rā′shən)**
   A growing worse; a gradual decline.
   The (di tir′ē ə rā′shən) of his health forced him
   to quit work.

7. **(pit′əns)**

A small amount of money or food.

He was paid a mere (pit′əns) for his hard day's work.

8. **(pôl′trē)**

Petty; of little value; worthless.

The millionaire was such a miser he gave only a (pôl′trē) fifty cents to the Red Cross.

9. **(tet′n əs)** or **(tet′nəs)**

A serious disease caused by bacteria that enter the body through a wound.

The doctor stitched Larry's wound and, as a precaution, gave him a (tet′n əs) shot.

10. **(snäb′ər ē)** or **(snäb′rē)**

Haughtiness; an act of looking down on people whom a person considers his or her inferiors.

We didn't like his (snäb′ər ē); he acted as if he were a genius and we were idiots.

---

1. **preliminary**
2. **turquoise**
3. **scrutiny**
4. **insurmountable**
5. **terminology**
6. **deterioration**
7. **pittance**
8. **paltry**
9. **tetanus**
10. **snobbery**

---

1. **(div′ət)**
   A piece of turf torn up by a golf stroke.
   I swung, missed the golf ball, and tore up a big
   (div′ət).

2. **(kùr′ē ər) or (kər′ē ər)**
   A person who carries official messages.
   A (kùr′ē ər) brought the general's message to the
   regiment's commander.

3. **(lik′wə dāt′)**
   To pay off or settle (a debt); to get rid of.
   He wanted to (lik′wə dāt′) his debts as soon as
   he had the money.

4. **(in′də lənt)**
   Lazy; habitually idle.
   Unlike his hard-working brother, he was an
   (in′də lənt) man.

5. **(sôr′əl)**
   Reddish brown; a reddish brown color.
   Susan's brown coat is a shade darker than the
   color of the (sôr′əl) horse she's riding.

6. **(ed′ē)**
   A small whirlpool or whirlwind.
   The canoe was caught in an (ed′ē) and spun
   around by the force of the stream.

7. **(pet′rə fī′)**
To stun with fear or surprise; to make lifeless or motionless as if turned into stone.
The sudden appearance of a cat seemed to (pet′rə fī′) the mouse.

8. **(pyü′trə fī′)**
To rot; to decay.
Fish and meat will (pyü′trə fī′) if not refrigerated.

9. **(pyü′trəd)**
Rotten; decayed.
The (pyü trəd) fish gave off a sickening smell.

10. **(tər′ni kət)** or **(tür′ni kət)**
A device used to stop temporarily the flow of blood through an artery.
The soldier made a (tər′ni kət) by twisting a handkerchief around his arm above the wound.

---

1. divot
2. courier
3. liquidate
4. indolent
5. sorrel
6. eddy
7. petrify
8. putrefy
9. putrid
10. tourniquet

---

1. **(kə līʹdə skōpʹ)**
   A tube containing colored glasses and mirrors
   showing a continually changing pattern as it turns.
   I turned the (kə līʹdə skōpʹ) and watched the
   colorful patterns change.

2. **(ärʹtə zən)**
   A person skilled in an applied art or in a trade; a
   craftsman.
   A talented (ärʹtə zən) created the stained-glass
   windows of the cathedral.

3. **(fabʹrə kātʹ)**
   To manufacture by assembling parts; to make.
   The company built a plant to (fabʹrə kātʹ)
   automobile engines.

4. **(tenʹyü əs)**
   Thin; slender; flimsy; weak.
   Spiders spin webs with (tenʹyü əs) threads.

5. **(yüʹfə mizʹəm)**
   A mild, indirect word or phrase used in place of
   one that sounds harsh, unpleasant, or offensive.
   A (yüʹfə mizʹəm) for *he died* is *he passed away.*

6. **(yü fōʹnē əs)**
   Pleasing in sound.
   The door bell chimed a (yü fōʹnē əs) melody.

---

7. **(yü′lə jīz′)**
   To praise highly.
   Many came to (yü′lə jīz′) the king at his
   funeral.

8. **(ik stōl′)** or **(ek stōl′)**
   To praise highly.
   We (ik stōl′) the Pilgrims for their courage and
   determination in seeking freedom.

9. **(lôd′ə tôr′ē)**
   Expressing praise.
   In his (lôd′ə tôr′ē) remarks the coach said that
   Dave was the best quarterback he'd ever
   coached.

10. **(ə blit′ə rāt′)**
    To destroy completely; to remove all traces of; to
    wipe out.
    Volcanic eruptions can (ə blit′ə rāt′) an entire
    city by burying it under mountains of ashes.

---

1. **kaleidoscope**
2. **artisan**
3. **fabricate**
4. **tenuous**
5. **euphemism**
6. **euphonious**
7. **eulogize**
8. **extol**
9. **laudatory**
10. **obliterate**

1. **(krēd′əns)**
   Belief; trustworthiness.
   I wouldn't give (krēd′əns) to that rumor.

2. **(krej′ə ləs)**
   Ready to believe; easily deceived.
   Sally was so (krej′ə ləs) that she believed every
   word the crooked salesman told her.

3. **(skep′ti kəl)**
   Doubting; not believing.
   "I'm (skep′ti kəl) about ghost stories because I've
   never seen a ghost."

4. **(ā′thē əst)**
   A person who doesn't believe in God.
   He was an (ā′thē əst) until he became a
   Christian.

5. **(ten′drəlz)**
   Slender, curly stems of climbing plants.
   Grapevine (ten′drəlz) cling to fences.

6. **(ôl′ tər kā′shən)**
   A noisy, angry dispute.
   The football coach got into an (ôl′tər kā′shən)
   with a referee over the penalty.

7. **(lir′ik)**
   Suitable for singing; expressing emotion.
   His (lir′ik) poem was made into a beautiful song.

8. **(līr)**
   An ancient musical instrument like a small harp.
   Apollo enchanted the Greek gods with the music of his (līr).

9. **(dal′yə) or (däl′yə)**
   A plant with large, bright-colored flowers.
   The (dal′yə) blooms in early autumn.

10. **(in′trə myür′əl)**
    Carried on by members of the same school.
    The freshmen beat the sophomores in the (in′trə myür′əl) softball game.

---

1. credence
2. credulous
3. skeptical
4. atheist
5. tendrils
6. altercation
7. lyric
8. lyre
9. dahlia
10. intramural

---

1. **(mə shet′ē)** or **(mə chet′ē)**
   A large, heavy knife used in Latin America.
   Swinging a (mə shet′ē), he cleared a path
   through the jungle.

2. **(ri plēt′)**
   Abundantly supplied; filled.
   This almanac is (ri plēt′) with valuable
   information.

3. **(has′əl)**
   An argument; a squabble.
   When I returned the faulty radio, the store
   manager refunded my money without a (has′əl).

4. **(dis kəm′fə chùr)** or **(dis kəm′fə chər)**
   Embarrassment; frustration.
   The coach's (dis kəm′fə chùr) was apparent as he
   paced the sideline watching his team lose.

5. **(val′ə dik′tər ē)**
   A farewell speech, especially one given at
   graduation exercises.
   The highest-ranking senior gave a five-minute
   (val′ə dik′tər ē) to end the graduation ceremony.

6. **(fes′təl)**
   Of a feast; joyous; festive.
   The royal wedding was a (fes′təl) occasion.

7. (här'bən jər)
   One that goes ahead to announce the coming of
   someone or something; a forerunner.
   The robin is a (här'bən jər) of spring.

8. (dis'taf)
   Female; of the maternal side of a family.
   Several ancestors on his (dis'taf) side fought for
   the Confederates in the Civil War.

9. (rō zet')
   An ornament made in the shape of a rose.
   She made a (rō zet') with red ribbons to use in
   wrapping Diana's gift.

10. (jel'ə tən)
    A jellylike substance made by boiling bones and
    other parts of animals.
    She made a dessert with fruit juices and
    (jel'ə tən).

---

1. machete
2. replete
3. hassle
4. discomfiture
5. valedictory
6. festal
7. harbinger
8. distaff
9. rosette
10. gelatin

---

1. **(ek′spə dīt′)**
   To speed up.
   He asked the shipping company to (ek′spə dīt′)
   the delivery.

2. **(ek′spə dish′əs)**
   Rapid and efficient; speedy.
   "Please send it by the most (ek′spə dish′əs)
   means possible."

3. **(ik spē′dē ənt) or (ek spē′dē ənt)**
   Suitable; serving to meet a need.
   He found it more (ik spē′dē ənt) to fly to New
   York than to drive.

4. **(äp′ər tün′) or (äp′ər tyün′)**
   Timely; suitable for a particular purpose.
   Jerry waited for an (äp′ər tün′) moment to ask
   for an increase in his allowance.

5. **(kôr′ə gā′təd) or (kär′ə gā′təd)**
   Formed into rows of ridges and grooves.
   (kôr′ə gā′təd) cardboard is used in packaging.

6. **(pēd′mänt)**
   Lying at the base of mountains.
   The thawing snow flooded rivers in the
   (pēd′mänt) valley.

7. **(və lēs′)**

   A small suitcase; a traveling bag.

   Katie packed her (və lēs′) for the slumber party.

8. **(hī drô′lik)**

   Operated by the force of liquid.

   Cars and trucks have (hī drô′lik) brakes that won't work if the fluid leaks out.

9. **(rō tənd′)**

   Round; plump.

   The snowman's (rō tənd′) body was made of a large snowball.

10. **(kən jēl′)**

    To thicken or harden; to stiffen from cold.

    The broth will (kən jēl′) into gelatin in the refrigerator.

---

1. **expedite**
2. **expeditious**
3. **expedient**
4. **opportune**
5. **corrugated**
6. **piedmont**
7. **valise**
8. **hydraulic**
9. **rotund**
10. **congeal**

---

1. **(tôr′pəd)**
   Sluggish; inactive.
   Lack of sleep made her as (tôr′pəd) as a
   hibernating bear.

2. **(tôr′pər)**
   Sluggishness; dullness.
   The bear was still in (tôr′pər) when it woke
   from its long winter's sleep.

3. **(lang′gwəd)**
   Sluggish; weak; drooping.
   The hot, humid weather made me too
   (lang′gwəd) to do any work.

4. **(lang′gər)**
   Sluggishness; weakness.
   "I was overcome by the (lang′gər) of the warm
   weather and didn't feel like doing work."

5. **(en′ər vā′ting)**
   Weakening; sapping the strength or vitality.
   Playing football in the hot and humid weather
   was (en′ər vā′ting).

6. **(lak′ə dā′zi kəl)**
   Lacking interest; halfhearted.
   (lak′ə dā′zi kəl) workers are not likely to get
   promotions.

7. **(vi vā′shəs)**

Lively; high-spirited.
A bunch of (vi vā′shəs) high school girls
jumped and cheered for their team.

8. **(kən viv′ē əl)**

Fond of parties with good company; jolly.
He enjoyed having dinners and parties with his
(kən viv′ē əl) friends.

9. **(mə rōs′)**

Ill-humored; gloomy.
Poor and sick, the (mə rōs′) old man cursed
fate for his misfortunes.

10. **(skər′mish)**

A brief battle between small groups of soldiers.
The border guards exchanged gunshots in the
(skər′mish).

---

1. torpid
2. torpor
3. languid
4. languor
5. enervating
6. lackadaisical
7. vivacious
8. convivial
9. morose
10. skirmish

---

1. **(tas′ət)**
   Understood but not openly expressed; not spoken or written; silent.
   He nodded in (tas′ət) consent to my plan.

2. **(tas′ə tərn′)**
   Habitually unwilling to talk; reserved in speech.
   That old farmer is (tas′ə tərn′), but his wife is talkative.

3. **(ret′ə sənt)**
   Inclined to be silent; reserved in speech.
   He is (ret′ə sənt) about what he plans to do with the money he has saved.

4. **(gar′ə ləs)**
   Talkative; talking too much about trifles.
   The (gar′ə ləs) old man bored everyone with his childhood stories.

5. **(lō kwā′shəs)**
   Talkative.
   She was (lō kwā′shəs) and talked for hours without letting anyone else speak.

6. **(väl′yə bəl)**
   Very talkative.
   She is so (väl′yə bəl) she will talk for hours if you let her.

7. **(sô tā′)** or **(sō tā′)**
   To fry quickly and lightly in a very small amount of fat; to panfry.
   "Slice and (sô tā′) the mushrooms in butter."

8. **(ə nē′mē ə)**
   An illness caused by lack of red blood cells.
   She was pale and weak from (ə nē′mē ə).

9. **(ə skans′)**
   With a side glance; suspiciously or disapprovingly.
   Cinderella's sisters looked (ə skans′) at her beautiful new dress.

10. **(lə nō′lē əm)** or **(li nō′lē əm)**
    A floor covering made of hard, washable material.
    Johnny tracked the kitchen (lə nō′lē əm) with his muddy boots.

---

1. **tacit**
2. **taciturn**
3. **reticent**
4. **garrulous**
5. **loquacious**
6. **voluble**
7. **saute**
8. **anemia**
9. **askance**
10. **linoleum**

---

1. **(kwiz′i kəl)**
   Puzzled; questioning.
   With a (kwiz′i kəl) look on her face, she asked
   for an explanation.

2. **(sin′thə səs)**
   The combination of parts to form a whole.
   Plastic is the result of chemical (sin′thə səs).

3. **(ə sī′ləm)**
   A place of safety or refuge; protection and refuge
   given to foreigners for political reasons.
   Seeking (ə sī′ləm) from persecution, the rebel
   leaders fled to neighboring countries.

4. **(rü′mə nənt)**
   Characterized by chewing cud.
   Some (rü′mə nənt) animals like cows and goats
   have a four-chambered stomach.

5. **(lar′ingks)**
   The upper part of the windpipe, containing the
   vocal cords.
   The (lar′ingks) is commonly called the voice box.

6. **(tē ar′ə), (tē er′ə), or (tē är′ə)**
   A woman's headband that looks like a small crown,
   often decorated with jewels or flowers.
   A diamond (tē ar′ə) sparkled in the queen's
   golden hair.

7. (sək singkt′)
   Clear and brief.
   Steve wrote a (sək singkt′) one-page report
   describing the highlights of his science project.

8. (tərs)
   Brief and to the point; concise.
   The general's (tərs) message said, "We won the
   battle."

9. (sə kā′də) or (sə kä′də)
   A large insect with transparent wings.
   A (sə kā′də) made a loud, shrill sound from the
   tree.

10. (ram′shak′əl)
    About to fall apart; loose and shaky.
    The (ram′shak′əl) old barn was blown down by
    the strong wind.

---

1. quizzical
2. synthesis
3. asylum
4. ruminant
5. larynx
6. tiara
7. succinct
8. terse
9. cicada
10. ramshackle

---

1. (skyü'ər)
   A pin of wood or metal for holding meat during cooking.
   She broiled diced beef, tomatoes, and onions on a bamboo (skyü'ər).

2. (rev'əl rē)
   Boisterous merrymaking.
   The locker room of the winning team was a scene of (rev'əl rē).

3. (dir'ə jə bəl) or (də rij' ə bəl)
   An airship; a large balloon that can be steered and driven by motors.
   A (dir'ə jə bəl) hovered over the stadium to take aerial pictures during the football game.

4. (ə flət'ər)
   Moving quickly with vibrations.
   The sails were (ə flət'ər) in the strong wind.

5. (hō'zhər ē)
   Stockings, socks, and related items.
   She bought stockings in the (hō'zhər ē) department of the store.

6. (mak'ər əl) or (mak'rəl)
   An ocean fish often used as food.
   The (mak'ər əl) looks like a small tuna.

7. **(dis krēt′)**
   Showing good judgment; cautious in words or action.
   A (dis krēt′) person would not tattle on his friends.

8. **(dis kresh′ən)**
   Freedom to decide or choose; good judgment.
   Selecting a picnic site was left to the (dis kresh′ən) of our club president.

9. **(wē′vəl)**
   A small beetle with a long snout.
   The (wē′vəl) does great harm to crops.

10. **(kē′äsk) or (kē äsk′)**
    A small building or stand with one or more open sides.
    He bought a magazine at the newspaper (kē′äsk) before catching a bus.

---

1. skewer
2. revelry
3. dirigible
4. aflutter
5. hosiery
6. mackerel
7. discreet
8. discretion
9. weevil
10. kiosk

---

1. **(pal′ət)**
   A narrow, hard bed; a mattress filled with straw.
   The poor old man slept on a straw (pal′ət).

2. **(pal′ət)**
   A thin board with a thumb hole, used by painters for holding and mixing colors.
   The artist mixed colors on his (pal′ət).

3. **(pal′ət)**
   a. The roof of the mouth.
   The child received treatment for a cleft (pal′ət).
   b. Taste.
   The food was a delight to his (pal′ət).

4. **(pal′ə tə bəl)**
   Agreeable to the taste.
   Finding nothing else (pal′ə tə bəl) on the menu, she ordered a hamburger.

5. **(pel′ət)**
   A small ball; a bullet.
   The man was hit in the leg by a shotgun (pel′ət).

6. **(kə lō′kwē əl)**
   Used in common talk; conversational; informal in speech.
   "Got a dime?" is a (kə lō′kwē əl) expression for "Have you a dime?"

7. **(riv′yə lət)**
   A small stream or brook.
   A (riv′yə lət) from the spring runs along the
   hiking trail.

8. **(dərj)**
   A funeral song.
   The choir sang a (dərj) at his funeral.

9. **(əb sôr′bənt) or (əb zôr′bənt)**
   Capable of soaking up something.
   This paper towel is so (əb sôr′bənt) it easily
   soaks up chocolate syrup.

10. **(ri zhēm′) or (rā zhēm′)**
    A government; a system of government.
    The people had no freedom under the military
    (ri zhēm′).

---

1. **pallet**
2. **palette**
3. **palate**
4. **palatable**
5. **pellet**
6. **colloquial**
7. **rivulet**
8. **dirge**
9. **absorbent**
10. **regime**

---

1. **(kär'trij)**
   A case filled with gun powder and a bullet or pellets.
   The soldier put another (kär'trij) in his rifle and fired.

2. **(kär'tl ij)** or **(kärt'lij)**
   A firm elastic tissue attached to bones near joints.
   The tip of the nose bone is flexible because it's formed of (kär'tl ij).

3. **(ri gāl')**
   To amuse; to entertain.
   He likes to (ri gāl') his friends with tales of his fishing trips.

4. **(ig zü'bər ənt)** or **(eg zü'bər ənt)**
   High-spirited; overflowing with cheer.
   The hometown fans gave their hero an (ig zü'bər ənt) welcome.

5. **(am fib'ē ən)**
   An animal that can live on land and in water.
   A frog is an (am fib'ē ən); it can live on land as well as in water.

6. **(gət'ər əl)**
   Sounded deep in the throat.
   He spoke with a (gət'ər əl) German accent.

7. **(sə lis′ət)**
   To ask earnestly; to make a request.
   Campaign workers (sə lis′ət) votes for their candidates.

8. **(sə lis′ə təs)**
   Concerned; anxious; eager.
   The (sə lis′ə təs) parents asked many questions about their children's school work.

9. **(kəl′mə nā′shən)**
   The highest point; climax.
   The fireworks display marked the (kəl′mə nā′shən) of daylong festivities on the Fourth of July.

10. **(stər′əp)**
    A ring that hangs from the horse's saddle to support the rider's foot.
    Gary stepped in the (stər′əp) and swung up onto the saddle.

---

1. **cartridge**
2. **cartilage**
3. **regale**
4. **exuberant**
5. **amphibian**
6. **guttural**
7. **solicit**
8. **solicitous**
9. **culmination**
10. **stirrup**

---

1. **(ig zôlt′)** or **(eg zôlt′)**
   To praise; to glorify.
   Worshipers (ig zôlt′) God by singing hymns.

2. **(ig zôrt′)** or **(eg zôrt′)**
   To urge strongly; to encourage.
   Cheerleaders (ig zôrt′) crowds to cheer their teams on.

3. **(ig zəlt′)** or **(eg zəlt′)**
   To rejoice greatly.
   Winners (ig zəlt′) in victory.

4. **(ig zəl′tənt)** or **(eg zəl′tənt)**
   Showing great joy; triumphant.
   The players gave an (ig zəl′tənt) shout and hugged each other after winning the game.

5. **(ka fēn′)** or **(kaf′ēn′)**
   A stimulating substance found in coffee and tea.
   The (ka fēn′) in coffee keeps her awake at night.

6. **(sə lil′ə kwē)**
   The act of talking to oneself; that which one says while talking to oneself.
   The actor uttered a (sə lil′ə kwē), pretending no one was there to hear him.

7. **(säl′ə tar′)** or **(säl′ə ter′)**
   a. A card game played by one person.
   He played (säl′ə tar′) in his room to pass the time.
   b. A precious stone set by itself.
   Her wedding ring is a one-carat diamond (säl′ə tar′).

8. **(flät′səm)**
   Floating wreckage of a ship.
   Rescuers found (flät′səm) but no survivors of the shipwreck.

9. **(ə pläm′)** or **(ə pləm′)**
   Self-assurance; poise.
   They asked her embarrassing questions, but she answered with (ə pläm′).

10. **(trüp)**
    A group of touring actors, singers, or other performers.
    He joined a circus (trüp) and traveled around the world with them.

---

1. **exalt**
2. **exhort**
3. **exult**
4. **exultant**
5. **caffeine** or **caffein**
6. **soliloquy**
7. **solitaire**
8. **flotsam**
9. **aplomb**
10. **troupe**

---

1. **(land′ləb′ər)**
   A landsman; a person not accustomed to life at sea.
   The new sailor was a (land′ləb′ər) who became seasick soon after the ship left shore.

2. **(pər sep′tə bəl)**
   Capable of being noticed.
   These two shades of red look so alike that the difference is hardly (pər sep′tə bəl).

3. **(tan′jə bəl)**
   Real; definite; capable of being touched.
   Bob's good grades were a (tan′jə bəl) sign of improvement in his studies.

4. **(ô then′tik)**
   Genuine; correct; trustworthy.
   The stories in his biography are (ô then′tik).

5. **(fôr′ā) or (fär′ā)**
   A raid for plunder; a sudden attack.
   The pirates made a (fôr′ā) on the coastal village.

6. **(trep′ə dā′shən)**
   Fear, alarm, or anxiety; a trembling from fear.
   Alice was seized with (trep′ə dā′shən) when she heard the weird noises in the haunted house.

---

7. **(kō ərs′)**
   To force; to compel.
   The hijacker used a gun to (kō ərs′) the pilot to fly to Cuba.

8. **(kō ər′shən)**
   The use of force to compel; force used to compel.
   The dictator could rule the people only by (kō ər′shən).

9. **(dù res′)** or **(dyù res′)**
   The use of force or threats to make someone do something he doesn't want to do.
   The prisoner signed a confession under (dù res′); he was threatened with death if he didn't.

10. **(tə nā′shəs)**
    Holding tightly; not giving up; tough.
    The bulldog's (tə nā′ shəs) jaws clung to the burglar's ankle.

---

1. **landlubber**
2. **perceptible**
3. **tangible**
4. **authentic**
5. **foray**
6. **trepidation**
7. **coerce**
8. **coercion**
9. **duress**
10. **tenacious**

---

1. **(mōv)**
   Pale purple.
   Lilacs have sweet-smelling (mōv) flowers.

2. **(in ter′ə gā′tər)**
   A person who examines by questioning.
   The cruel (in ter′ə gā′tər) beat his prisoners
   when their answers didn't suit him.

3. **(in tə räg′ə tiv)**
   Asking a question; expressing a question.
   (in tə räg′ə tiv) sentences should end with
   question marks.

4. **(kash)**
   A hidden treasure or supply; a hiding place for
   treasure or supplies.
   The pirates had a (kash) of gold and jewels in a
   cave on the island.

5. **(vī′nəl)** or **(vīn′l)**
   A kind of tough plastic.
   Many phonograph records are made of (vī′nəl).

6. **(lin′ə mənt)**
   An oily medicine for rubbing on the skin to ease
   aches or pain.
   The doctor gave him a (lin′ə mənt) to rub on
   his bruised leg.

7. **(dis′ə dənt)**
   Not agreeing, as in political or religious belief.
   The (dis′ə dənt) group held an anti-war
   demonstration.

8. **(her′ə sē)**
   An opinion different from accepted belief.
   Because Einstein's theories were completely new
   and different, they were considered (her′ə sē) by
   other scientists.

9. **(chər′lish)**
   Rude; bad-tempered; uncivil in speech; ill-bred.
   His (chər′lish) manners displeased the hostess.

10. **(ves′tij)**
    A trace, a mark, or a sign left by something that
    has disappeared.
    No (ves′tij) of the house could be found after
    the big flood.

---

1. **mauve**
2. **interrogator**
3. **interrogative**
4. **cache**
5. **vinyl**
6. **liniment**
7. **dissident**
8. **heresy**
9. **churlish**
10. **vestige**

---

1. (i mā'shē ā'təd)
   Thin and wasted.
   Pale and (i mā'shē ā'təd), the starved man
   looked like a scarecrow.

2. (kə dav'ər əs)
   Pale and thin; of or like a dead person.
   Starved and sick, the man looked (kə dav'ər əs).

3. (ə sən'dər)
   Apart; in pieces.
   Dynamite blasted the building (ə sən'dər).

4. (də min'yə tiv)
   Very small.
   Janet's dollhouse has five rooms filled with
   (də min'yə tiv) furniture.

5. (fə sē'shəs)
   Amusing; intended to be humorous.
   Her (fə sē'shəs) remarks were inappropriate for
   such a solemn occasion.

6. (tô'nē)
   Light brown.
   The lion had a black mane and a (tô'nē) coat of
   short hair.

The Spelling Bee Speller

7. **(ät′ə mən)**
   A low, cushioned footstool.
   He sat in an armchair with his feet propped up
   on an (ät′ə mən).

8. **(has′ək)**
   A firm cushion used as a footstool or a seat.
   Amy sat on the (has′ək) next to her father's
   armchair.

9. **(pil′ij)**
   The act of looting or plundering.
   The (pil′ij) by the bandits left the town in
   ruins.

10. **(ang′kər man′)**
    A newscaster who coordinates news stories offered
    by other reporters.
    The television (ang′kər man′) read news stories
    reported from all over the world.

---

1. **emaciated**
2. **cadaverous**
3. **asunder**
4. **diminutive**
5. **facetious**
6. **tawny**
7. **ottoman**
8. **hassock**
9. **pillage**
10. **anchorman**

---

1. **(pret′səl)**
   A hard, salted biscuit shaped like a knot or a stick.
   I had a hot (pret′səl) and a glass of milk for a snack.

2. **(vī′kount′)**
   A nobleman ranking above a baron and below an earl.
   The king made him a nobleman by granting him the title of (vī′kount′).

3. **(par′ə mount′)**
   Above all others; chief in importance.
   The doctor's (par′ə mount′) concern was to save his patient's life.

4. **(fas′əl)**
   Easy; done effortlessly.
   We have no (fas′əl) solutions to these complex problems.

5. **(nik′nak′)**
   A small ornament; a trinket.
   Amy put the toy soldier on her (nik′nak′) shelf.

6. **(bô′bəl)**
   A child's toy; something showy having little value.
   Betsy won a (bô′bəl) as a door prize at the party.

7. **(plô′zə bəl)**
   Seemingly true or reasonable.
   What he says sounds (plô′zə bəl), but I don't
   think it's really true.

8. **(fē′zə bəl)**
   Capable of being done; possible.
   His method of using solar energy is technically
   (fē′zə bəl) but will cost many extra millions of
   dollars.

9. **(gōrd)** or **(gôrd)**
   A fruit that grows on a vine and has a hard shell.
   We made bowls from dried (gōrd) shells.

10. **(spə rad′ik)**
    Scattered; happening from time to time.
    The speaker was interrupted several times by the
    (spə rad′ik) booing and jeering of the crowd.

---

1. **pretzel**
2. **viscount**
3. **paramount**
4. **facile**
5. **knickknack**
6. **bauble**
7. **plausible**
8. **feasible**
9. **gourd**
10. **sporadic**

---

1. **(äb sesh′ən)** or **(əb sesh′ən)**
   An idea that takes over one's mind; a haunting idea or feeling.
   Driving race cars became an (äb sesh′ən) with Jim.

2. **(fet′ish)** or **(fē′tish)**
   Something to which too much attention or devotion is given; a thing that is believed to have magic power.
   By making a (fet′ish) of weight control, she nearly starved to death.

3. **(am′yə lət)**
   A charm worn to ward off evil or to bring good luck.
   Julie carried a rabbit's foot as an (am′yə lət) for success in the spelling bee.

4. **(tal′is mən)** or **(tal′iz mən)**
   A good luck charm; something that has magical power.
   Aladdin's lamp was a (tal′is mən) that let him have anything he wished.

5. **(bī lat′ər əl)**
   Affecting or binding two sides.
   The two armies reached a (bī lat′ər əl) agreement to withdraw from the battle zone.

6. **(kə lat′ər əl)**
   Security for a loan.
   When he borrowed money at the bank, he used his car as (kə lat′ər əl).

7. **(kwôrts)**
   A clear, hard mineral found in sand or other rocks.
   (kwôrts) is often found in clear six-sided crystals.

8. **(ə kred′ə təd)**
   Approved officially; recognized as satisfying an official standard.
   This medical school is (ə kred′ə təd) for training doctors.

9. **(pen′ə təns)**
   Sorrow or regret for one's wrongdoing.
   The thief showed his (pen′ə təns) and promised never to steal again.

10. **(pen′ə ten′shər ē) or (pen′ə ten′chər ē)**
    A prison for those who have committed serious crimes.
    A prisoner escaped the (pen′ə ten′shər ē) by climbing over a wall.

---

1. **obsession**
2. **fetish**
3. **amulet**
4. **talisman**
5. **bilateral**
6. **collateral**
7. **quartz**
8. **accredited**
9. **penitence**
10. **penitentiary**

1. **(di myùr′)**
   Quiet, modest, or shy.
   Julie is a (di myùr′) country girl, but her sister is a tomboy.

2. **(di mər′)**
   Objection; hesitation.
   Without (di mər′), he agreed to work overtime.

3. **(ak sēd′)**
   a. To agree; to consent.
   To avoid a lengthy strike, the owner had to (ak sēd′) to the workers' demand.
   b. To take an office; to succeed.
   The prince will (ak sēd′) to the throne when the king passes away.

4. **(kôr′ə nər)** or **(kär′ə nər)**
   A public official whose job is to find out the cause of any violent or unnatural death.
   The (kôr′ə nər) said the man did not drown but was shot to death, then thrown into the lake.

5. **(dī′ə krit′i kəl)**
   Serving to distinguish among sounds in spoken language.
   The (dī′ə krit′i kəl) mark shows that the word *ape* (āp) is pronounced with a long vowel.

6. **(tas′əl)**
   A hanging ornament made of a bunch of threads or cords tied together at one end and loose at the other.
   The cap worn at graduation ceremonies has a flat square top with a (tas′əl).

7. **(skwäl'əd)**
Dirty; filthy; miserable.
Piles of garbage lined the streets of the (skwäl'əd) neighborhood.

8. **(skwäl'ər)**
Filth; misery.
The poor families lived in the crowded (skwäl'ər) of the slums.

9. **(sôr'dəd)**
Filthy; squalid.
The prisoners' (sôr'dəd) quarters looked like pigsties.

10. **(tüt'əl ij)** or **(tyüt'əl ij)**
Guardianship; instruction.
Under his (tüt'əl ij) she soon became a skilled pianist.

---

1. demure
2. demur
3. accede
4. coroner
5. diacritical
6. tassel
7. squalid
8. squalor
9. sordid
10. tutelage

---

1. (ôr′thə dän′təst)
   A dentist who specializes in the correction of abnormally positioned teeth.
   Because Amy's teeth were crooked, she went to an (ôr′thə dän′təst) to get braces.

2. (ôr′thə däks′)
   Holding to traditional or established beliefs or doctrines.
   Darwin's theory of evolution didn't agree with the (ôr′thə däks′) views of the church.

3. (fər′vər)
   Great warmth of feeling; passion.
   In an outpouring of patriotic (fər′vər), many people volunteered to fight in the war.

4. (rü′də men′tər ē) or (rü′də men′trē)
   Elementary.
   You need some (rü′də men′tər ē) knowledge of music to play the piano.

5. (lim′ər ik)
   A humorous five-line poem.
   The children burst into laughter when they read the (lim′ər ik).

6. (sə rinj′)
   A medical tool for injecting fluids into the body or for drawing blood out of the body.
   The nurse used a long-needled (sə rinj′) to take a blood sample from my arm.

7. **(frô′jə lənt)**
   Cheating; dishonest.
   It is (frô′jə lənt) to pay by check when no
   money is left in one's bank account.

8. **(em bez′əl mənt)**
   The act of stealing money entrusted to one's care.
   The bank teller fled the country with the money
   before the (em bez′əl mənt) was discovered.

9. **(môrg)**
   A place where bodies of dead persons are kept
   until identified or buried.
   The bodies of the accident victims were taken to
   a hospital (môrg).

10. **(həb′əb)**
    A loud, confused noise; an uproar.
    He had to shout to make himself heard above
    the (həb′əb) of traffic.

---

1. **orthodontist**
2. **orthodox**
3. **fervor**
4. **rudimentary**
5. **limerick**
6. **syringe**
7. **fraudulent**
8. **embezzlement**
9. **morgue**
10. **hubbub**

---

1. **(kən cher′tō)**
   A musical composition for one or more solo instruments with the accompaniment of an orchestra.
   Julie rehearsed the piano (kən cher′tō) with the orchestra.

2. **(rek′lüs) or (ri klüs′)**
   A person who lives alone and avoids the company of others.
   The millionaire (rek′lüs) hasn't been seen in public for ten years.

3. **(lē′ə zän′) or (lē ā′zän′)**
   A person who aids communication between groups of people; a means of maintaining communication.
   During the war, the general served as an American (lē′ə zän′) with British troops in Europe.

4. **(ig züd′) or (eg züd′)**
   To send out in small drops; to give off as if by oozing.
   In the spring maple trees (ig züd′) sap that can be collected and cooked to make syrup.

5. **(fal′ə sē)**
   A false or misleading idea.
   It's a (fal′ə sē) to suppose that if you are rich, you are happy.

6. **(fə lā′shəs)**
   Misleading; faulty in reasoning.
   The argument that cigarette smoking doesn't harm health has been proven (fə lā′shəs).

---

7. (sīz′mə graf′) or (sīs′mə graf′)

An instrument that shows when and where an earthquake happens and how powerful it is.
A (sīz′mə graf′) can record earthquake tremors occurring thousands of miles away.

8. (en kəm′brəns) or (in kəm′brəns)

A burden; something that hinders.
Too much equipment is an (en kəm′brəns) on a camping trip.

9. (klan des′tən)

Secret; done secretly.
The spies held (klan des′tən) meetings to avoid being noticed by police.

10. (pik′chə resk′)

Like a picture; suitable for a painting.
Switzerland is famous for its (pik′chə resk′) mountains and valleys.

---

1. concerto
2. recluse
3. liaison
4. exude
5. fallacy
6. fallacious
7. seismograph
8. encumbrance
9. clandestine
10. picturesque

---

1. **(mal'ə dik'shən)**
   A curse.
   The wicked witch screamed a (mal'ə dik'shən) at Dorothy.

2. **(mə lev'ə lənt)**
   Wishing harm or evil to others.
   The robber had a (mə lev'ə lənt) look on his face as he pointed a gun at the cashier.

3. **(rang'kər)**
   Bitter resentment; ill will.
   The man was full of (rang'kər) against the judge who sent him to prison for a crime he didn't commit.

4. **(an'ə mäs'ə tē)**
   Deep hatred; intense dislike.
   The (an'ə mäs'ə tē) between the two boys led to a fist fight.

5. **(kən käk'shən)**
   Something made by mixing or combining ingredients, as in stew.
   She cooked a (kən käk'shən) of meat and vegetables and called it chop suey.

6. **(skab'ərd)**
   A case in which the blade of a sword or of a dagger is kept.
   The pirate drew his sword from the (skab'ərd) hanging at his side.

7. **(ag′rə vāt′)**
To make worse; to irritate.
Scratching mosquito bites will only (ag′rə vāt′)
the itch.

8. **(ig zas′pə rā′shən)** or **(eg zas′pə rā′shən)**
Irritation; annoyance.
In (ig zas′pə rā′shən), the speaker refused to
answer any more interrupting questions.

9. **(sem′ə fôr′)**
A visual signaling system or device with flags,
lights, or mechanically moving arms.
The (sem′ə fôr′) at the railroad crossing flashed
yellow, warning trains to slow down.

10. **(mem′ər ə bil′ē ə)** or **(mem′ər ə bil′yə)**
Things worth remembering.
Her scrapbook is full of pictures and other
childhood (mem′ər ə bil′ē ə).

---

1. **malediction**
2. **malevolent**
3. **rancor**
4. **animosity**
5. **concoction**
6. **scabbard**
7. **aggravate**
8. **exasperation**
9. **semaphore**
10. **memorabilia**

---

1. **(mə naj′ər ē)**
   A place where wild animals are kept in cages for exhibition.
   We saw lions and elephants at the circus (mə naj′ər ē).

2. **(vô rā′shəs) or (və rā′shəs)**
   Eager or greedy in eating.
   The long afternoon hike gave the children (vô rā′shəs) appetites.

3. **(rav′ə nəs)**
   Very hungry; very greedy.
   The (rav′ə nəs) wolves began eating the moose even before it was dead.

4. **(in sā′shə bəl) or (in sā′shē ə bəl)**
   Incapable of being satisfied.
   He had an (in sā′shə bəl) hunger for knowledge, which made him want to read all the books he could find.

5. **(sā′shē ā′təd)**
   Satisfied fully; filled to excess.
   We ate candy until we were (sā′shē ā′təd).

6. **(sər′fət)**
   An excessive amount or supply.
   The children had a (sər′fət) of candy after the Halloween party.

7. **(jet′ə sən)** or **(jet′ə zən)**
   To throw overboard; to discard.
   They had to (jet′ə sən) the cargo when the ship
   began to sink.

8. **(väl′ə təl)**
   Evaporating quickly; changeable; unstable.
   Gasoline is a (väl′ə təl) and flammable liquid.

9. **(sin′yü ē)**
   Strong; tough.
   Dave has the (sin′yü ē) legs of a marathon
   runner.

10. **(nü mat′ik)** or **(nyü mat′ik)**
    Of air; filled with air.
    The air in (nü mat′ik) tires works like a
    cushion, making them more comfortable to ride
    on than solid rubber tires.

---

1. **menagerie**
2. **voracious**
3. **ravenous**
4. **insatiable**
5. **satiated**
6. **surfeit**
7. **jettison**
8. **volatile**
9. **sinewy**
10. **pneumatic**

---

1. **(yō′mən)**

   A petty officer assigned to clerical duties in the United States Navy.

   She began her Navy career as a (yō′mən).

2. **(mēn)**

   One's bearing, manner, or appearance.

   President Woodrow Wilson had the (mēn) of a college professor.

3. **(di mē′nər)**

   The way a person behaves.

   The judge's calm (di mē′nər) helped restore peace in the courtroom.

4. **(mis′di mē′nər)**

   A minor crime.

   Running a red light is a (mis′di mē′nər) usually punishable by a fine.

5. **(fel′ə nē)**

   A serious crime.

   Burglary is a (fel′ə nē) punishable by imprisonment.

6. **(di tər′ənt)**

   Something that prevents or discourages.

   A strong police force is a (di tər′ənt) to crime.

---

7. (pik′ə lō′)
A small flute.
The (pik′ə lō′) is smaller in size and higher in pitch than a regular flute.

8. (mäsk)
A Moslem temple.
The (mäsk) has a tall, slender tower from which criers call people to prayer.

9. (i man′sə pā′shən)
The act of setting free from slavery or bondage. President Lincoln proclaimed the (i man′sə pā′shən) of all slaves, making them free in the South as well as in the North.

10. (lik′ər əs), (lik′ər ish) or (lik′rish)
A chewy candy flavored with a sweet, strong-tasting juice extracted from the root of a plant. Johnny likes to chew (lik′ər əs) sticks.

---

1. yeoman
2. mien
3. demeanor
4. misdemeanor
5. felony
6. deterrent
7. piccolo
8. mosque
9. emancipation
10. licorice

---

1. **(nig′ərd lē)**
   Meanly small; stingy; meager.
   After eating a full course dinner, the customer
   left only a (nig′ərd lē) tip.

2. **(mag nan′ə məs)**
   Very generous; free from petty feelings; forgiving.
   It was (mag nan′ə məs) of the general to treat
   his defeated enemy so kindly.

3. **(shiv′əl rəs)**
   Valiant; courteous; generous.
   A (shiv′əl rəs) knight went to rescue the maiden.

4. **(jen′ə səs)**
   The origin; the beginning; creation.
   The first book in the Bible is about the
   (jen′ə səs) of Israel.

5. **(käm′ən dir′)**
   To take by force; to seize for military or police
   use.
   To chase a fleeing robber, the police had to
   (käm′ən dir′) a taxi.

6. **(dā′byü′) or (dā′byü′)**
   A first public appearance; the formal introduction
   of a young woman to society.
   He made his (dā′byü′) as a concert pianist at
   age seventeen.

7. **(rē′hə bil′ə tā′shən)**
   Restoration to useful life by training or therapy.
   The (rē′hə bil′ə tā′shən) program helped him
   learn to walk with artificial legs.

8. **(in′əd vər′tnt)**
   Careless; unintentional.
   It was an (in′əd vər′tnt) mistake; I should have
   added the numbers instead of subtracting.

9. **(ap′ə thē)**
   Lack of interest; indifference.
   Voter (ap′ə thē) was blamed for the low
   turnout on election day.

10. **(las′ə rā′shən)**
    A roughly torn wound; a jagged tear.
    The (las′ə rā′shən) on his finger from a dog
    bite needed three stitches.

---

1. **niggardly**
2. **magnanimous**
3. **chivalrous**
4. **genesis**
5. **commandeer**
6. **debut**
7. **rehabilitation**
8. **inadvertent**
9. **apathy**
10. **laceration**

---

1. **(di kliv′ə tē)**
   A downward slope.
   The smooth, long (di kliv′ə tē) of that hill is
   ideal for skiing.

2. **(səf′rij)**
   The right to vote.
   It was not until 1920 that American women
   received (səf′rij).

3. **(jär′gən)**
   The specialized language used in a trade or a
   profession.
   The lawyer spoke in plain English without using
   legal (jär′gən).

4. **(pär′ləns)**
   A way of speaking; language.
   In computer (pär′ləns), a *bug* is an error in a
   computer program.

5. **(ə vərd′)**
   Declared firmly and confidently.
   The witness (ə vərd′) that the suspect was the
   gunman who robbed the bank.

6. **(ik strav′ə gəns)** or **(ek strav′ə gəns)**
   The wasteful spending of money.
   A new mink coat was an (ik strav′ə gəns) for
   the young waitress.

7. (rəs′ət)
   Reddish brown.
   Maple leaves turn gold and (rəs′ət) in the
   autumn.

8. (el′ə jē)
   A song or poem expressing sorrow for the dead.
   The poet wrote an (el′ə jē) for the king's
   funeral.

9. (ə spar′ə gəs)
   A plant whose tender shoots are used for food.
   Young (ə spar′ə gəs) cooked and served with
   butter is delicious.

10. (klī′ən tel′)
    A body of customers.
    The lawyer had a large (klī′ən tel′) among the
    town's businessmen.

---

1. declivity
2. suffrage
3. jargon
4. parlance
5. averred
6. extravagance
7. russet
8. elegy
9. asparagus
10. clientele

---

1. **(dis bərs′)**
   To pay out.
   The job of a paymaster is to (dis bərs′) salaries and wages.

2. **(rē′im bərs′)**
   To pay back.
   His employer will (rē′im bərs′) him for airline tickets and other travel expenses.

3. **(in dem′nə fī′)**
   To make up for loss or damage.
   The insurance company will (in dem′nə fī′) the homeowner in case of fire or theft.

4. **(rek′əm pens′)**
   A payment; a reward.
   Your thanks are enough (rek′əm pens′) for my effort.

5. **(ri sip′rə kāt′)**
   To do or give in return; to return in kind.
   "I'd like to (ri sip′rə kāt′) your favor; please let me know if you need anything."

6. **(aj′ə lā′shən)**
   Praise; flattery.
   The singer won the (aj′ə lā′shən) of teenage fans, who sent him flowers, letters, and gifts.

7. **(sə sep′tə bəl)**
   Easily affected or influenced.
   Cigarette smoking makes people (sə sep′tə bəl)
   to lung and heart disease.

8. **(res′pət)**
   A period of rest or relief.
   The brief rainstorm gave us a welcome (res′pət)
   from the scorching heat.

9. **(ləg zhùr′ē ənt) or (lək shùr′ē ənt)**
   Growing abundantly; lush.
   A (ləg zhùr′ē ənt) growth of trees covered the
   entire jungle.

10. **(səmp′chü əs)**
    Lavish; luxurious; costly.
    The king entertained his guests with a
    (səmp′chü əs) dinner of the finest food and
    wine.

---

1. **disburse**
2. **reimburse**
3. **indemnify**
4. **recompense**
5. **reciprocate**
6. **adulation**
7. **susceptible**
8. **respite**
9. **luxuriant**
10. **sumptuous**

---

1. **(ri səs′ə tāt′)**
   To revive; to bring back to life.
   The lifeguard used artificial respiration to
   (ri səs′ə tāt′) the drowned man.

2. **(in sər′jənt)**
   Rebellious; rising in revolt.
   The (in sər′jənt) forces took control of the
   town's radio station.

3. **(in′sə rek′shən)**
   A rebellion; a revolt.
   The army moved in to put down the
   (in′sə rek′shən).

4. **(si dish′əs)**
   Stirring up discontent or rebellion.
   Anyone suspected of (si dish′əs) writing or
   speeches was sent to prison by the dictator.

5. **(i lips′)**
   A closed curve that looks like a flattened circle; an
   oval.
   That football stadium is shaped like an (i lips′).

6. **(rez′ə dü′)** or **(rez′ə dyü′)**
   Something left after a main part has been taken
   away.
   Ash is the grayish-white powdery (rez′ə dü′) after
   something has been burned.

---

7. **(dī'ə bäl'ik)**
   Devilish; very wicked.
   The witch had a (dī'ə bäl'ik) scheme to trick
   Hansel and Gretel.

8. **(fēn'dish)**
   Like a devil; very wicked or cruel.
   The (fēn'dish) kidnappers killed the hostages
   before making their getaway.

9. **(lak'ər)**
   A clear varnish.
   That tray has a shiny (lak'ər) finish.

10. **(sil'ü et')**
    An outline of an object, filled in with a solid
    color, usually black.
    We saw the mountains in (sil'ü et') against the
    misty morning sky.

---

1. **resuscitate**
2. **insurgent**
3. **insurrection**
4. **seditious**
5. **ellipse**
6. **residue**
7. **diabolic**
8. **fiendish**
9. **lacquer**
10. **silhouette**

1. (ə bäm'ə nə bəl)
    Very bad; very unpleasant; hateful.
    The food at the restaurant was (ə bäm'ə nə bəl);
    the soup was cold and the steak was tough.

2. (hā'nəs)
    Very wicked; hateful.
    Kidnapping and murdering are (hā'nəs) crimes.

3. (ō'dē əs)
    Hateful; disgusting.
    Spending a night in jail was an (ō'dē əs)
    experience for him.

4. (ə trō'shəs)
    Very wicked or cruel; savage and brutal.
    The prisoners received (ə trō'shəs) treatment;
    many of them were starved or beaten to death.

5. (ə träs'ə tē)
    A very wicked or cruel act.
    The terrorists committed one (ə träs'ə tē) after
    another; they bombed buildings and killed people.

6. (shär'lə tən)
    One who pretends to have knowledge or skill; a
    quack; an imposter.
    The (shär'lə tən) pretended to be a doctor and
    sold them a fake cure-all.

7. **(ri vər′bə rāt′)**
To echo back.
I heard their voices (ri vər′bə rāt′) in the cave.

8. **(kən vər′sənt)**
Familiar; well-informed.
A referee must be (kən vər′sənt) with the rules of the game.

9. **(al′ə gôr′ē)**
A story in which characters are used as symbols for teaching and explaining.
John Bunyan wrote the famous (al′ə gôr′ē) *Pilgrim's Progress.*

10. **(fi zēk′)**
The body; the appearance of the body.
Tall and strong, Gary has the (fi zēk′) of a football player.

1. abominable
2. heinous
3. odious
4. atrocious
5. atrocity
6. charlatan
7. reverberate
8. conversant
9. allegory
10. physique

1. **(thrōz)**
   Agony; painful struggle.
   The nation was in the (thrōz) of a great civil war.

2. **(lāt′nt)**
   Hidden; present but not developed or brought out.
   Our (lāt′nt) desires and worries are often revealed in dreams.

3. **(em′brē ō′)**
   An organism in a very early stage of development.
   A chicken inside an egg is an (em′brē ō′).

4. **(gə ril′ə)**
   A member of a small group of fighters carrying on irregular warfare.
   (gə ril′ə) attacks greatly harassed the occupying army.

5. **(jəng′kət)**
   A pleasure trip.
   The Congressman went on a (jəng′kət) to Africa at the taxpayers' expense.

6. **(in′fə məs)**
   Having a very bad reputation; notorious.
   Benedict Arnold will go down in American history as an (in′fə məs) traitor.

7. **(ig′nə min′ē əs)**
Disgraceful; humiliating.
The baseball team lost the game by the
(ig′nə min′ē əs) score of 35-0.

8. **(des′pi kə bəl)** or **(di spik′ə bəl)**
Deserving to be scorned as wicked or cruel.
Betraying a friend is a (des′pi kə bəl) act.

9. **(rü′bärb)**
A plant with large leaves and long stalks, used in cooking.
She cooked (rü′bärb) stalks to make a pie filling.

10. **(ek′spər tēz′)**
Expert skill; know-how.
To become a good surgeon requires (ek′spər tēz′).

1. throes
2. latent
3. embryo
4. guerrilla or guerilla
5. junket
6. infamous
7. ignominious
8. despicable
9. rhubarb
10. expertise

1. **(lat′əs)**

   A framework made of crossed strips of wood or metal with open spaces between them.

   We put a (lat′əs) in front of the screen to keep our dog from scratching holes in it.

2. **(koun′tə nəns)**

   The face.

   His stern (koun′tə nəns) brightened when he heard the good news.

3. **(sab′əth)**

   The day of the week set aside for rest and worship.

   She rarely misses going to church on the (sab′əth).

4. **(an′əs thet′ik)**

   A drug that makes the body feel no pain.

   I felt no pain when the dentist pulled my tooth because he used an (an′əs thet′ik).

5. **(fyüd′l)**

   Of the political and social system of Europe in the Middle Ages.

   Under the (fyüd′l) system the king granted land to his knights in return for their military service.

6. **(vas′əl)**

   A person in the Middle Ages who offered loyalty and service to a lord in return for protection or for use of land.

   In medieval England a knight who served a king was the king's (vas′əl).

7. **(i nō′bəl)** or **(e nō′bəl)**
   To make noble or honorable.
   Helping others in need does (i nō′bəl) the helper.

8. **(kôr′ə lā′shən)** or **(kär′ə lā′shən)**
   A relationship.
   A close (kôr′ə lā′shən) usually exists between a person's height and weight.

9. **(pē′kənt)**
   Pleasantly stimulating to the taste; sharp.
   The (pē′kənt) Kosher pickles made my mouth pucker.

10. **(pən′jənt)**
    Sharp and stinging to the senses of taste or smell.
    The (pən′jənt) smell of burning leaves made me sneeze.

---

1. **lattice**
2. **countenance**
3. **Sabbath**
4. **anesthetic** or **anaesthetic**
5. **feudal**
6. **vassal**
7. **ennoble**
8. **correlation**
9. **piquant**
10. **pungent**

---

1. **(ig zil′ə rā′ting)** or **(eg zil′ə rā′ting)**
   Cheering; making lively; refreshing.
   I found it (ig zil′ə rā′ting) to walk through the
   park in the brisk morning air.

2. **(näm′ə nəl)**
   Very small; in name only.
   The students paid a (näm′ə nəl) fee of fifty cents
   to see the movie at school.

3. **(vər′chü əl)**
   Real in effect but not in fact or name.
   Since the army lost so many soldiers, their
   victory was a (vər′chü əl) defeat.

4. **(grə nād′)**
   A small bomb usually thrown by hand.
   The soldier threw a (grə nād′) that set off a
   loud explosion.

5. **(big′ə təd)**
   Prejudiced; narrow-minded; unwilling to allow
   opinions or customs different from one's own.
   He was (big′ə təd) and wouldn't listen to anyone
   who disagreed with him.

6. **(sə nar′ē ō′)** or **(sə ner′ē ō′)**
   An outline of an event, a play, or a motion
   picture.
   The actress spent days studying her (sə nar′ē ō′).

7. **(ī tin′ə rer′ē)** or **(ə tin′ə rer′ē)**
   A plan of travel; a list of places to visit on a journey.
   Their (ī tin′ə rer′ē) included a two-day stop in Paris, France.

8. **(ī tin′ər ənt)** or **(ə tin′ər ənt)**
   Traveling from place to place.
   The farmer hired (ī tin′ər ənt) workers during the harvest season.

9. **(fôrt)** or **(fôr′tā)**
   A strong point; a special talent; something a person does particularly well.
   Larry plays several musical instruments, but his (fôrt) is the piano.

10. **(fiz′ə səst)**
    A scientist who deals with matter, energy, motion, and related subjects.
    Albert Einstein, the great (fiz′ə səst) and mathematician, developed important theories related to the speed of light.

---

1. **exhilarating**
2. **nominal**
3. **virtual**
4. **grenade**
5. **bigoted**
6. **scenario**
7. **itinerary**
8. **itinerant**
9. **forte**
10. **physicist**

1. **(gri gar′ē əs)** or **(gri ger′ē əs)**
   Living in flocks or herds; sociable; fond of company.
   Sheep are (gri gar′ē əs) animals; they always flock together when they graze.

2. **(skəl′ər ē)**
   A room next to a kitchen, used for cleaning utensils and for washing vegetables.
   She washed dishes and pans in the (skəl′ər ē) all morning.

3. **(bi kwēth′)** or **(bi kwēth′)**
   To give by a will; to hand down.
   The rich widow decided to (bi kwēth′) her mansion to an orphanage.

4. **(mô′sə lē′əm)** or **(mô′zə lē′əm)**
   A stone building housing a tomb or tombs.
   His coffin was placed next to his father's in the family (mô′sə lē′əm).

5. **(di kôr′əm)** or **(di kōr′əm)**
   Proper behavior; good taste.
   The judge told the noisy spectators to act with (di kôr′əm) in his court.

6. **(snôr′kəl)**
   A tube used by swimmers for breathing underwater.
   The skin diver breathed through a (snôr′kəl).

7. **(bə lij′ər ənt)**
   Eager to fight; hostile.
   The (bə lij′ər ənt) bully always tried to pick
   fights with smaller boys.

8. **(kən ten′shəs)**
   Quarrelsome; tending to argue or dispute.
   The (kən ten′shəs) coach protested every time
   his team was penalized.

9. **(pəg nā′shəs)**
   Fond of fighting; quick to fight.
   Wild boars are (pəg nā′shəs) animals; they will
   put up a stiff fight if attacked.

10. **(ek′sə jən sē)**
    A situation that requires quick action, attention, or
    aid.
    Firemen had to be called for the (ek′sə jən sē).

---

1. **gregarious**
2. **scullery**
3. **bequeath**
4. **mausoleum**
5. **decorum**
6. **snorkel**
7. **belligerent**
8. **contentious**
9. **pugnacious**
10. **exigency**

---

1. **(kən dō′ləns)**
   An expression of sympathy.
   The general sent a letter of (kən dō′ləns) to the dead soldier's widow.

2. **(säl′əs)**
   Comfort in grief or misfortune.
   In the company of her friends she found (säl′əs) from her sorrow.

3. **(səs′tə nəns)**
   Means of support; food; livelihood.
   Fish and seals are the main source of (səs′tə nəns) for the Eskimos.

4. **(et′ə mäl′ə jē)**
   The origin and history of a word.
   The word *sandwich* has an interesting (et′ə mäl′ə jē); it was named after the Earl of Sandwich.

5. **(frə net′ik)**
   Frenzied; frantic.
   The crew made (frə net′ik) efforts to save the sinking ship.

6. **(ap′ə rat′əs)** or **(ap′ə rā′təs)**
   Equipment or tools used for a particular purpose.
   The (ap′ə rat′əs) used for breathing by skin divers is called a snorkel.

7. **(də lap'ə dā'təd)**
   Partly ruined or decayed; falling to pieces.
   The (də lap'ə dā'təd) old house had a leaky
   roof and chipped plaster walls.

8. **(di krep'ət)**
   Old and worn out; broken down by old age.
   He sold his (di krep'ət) car to a junkyard.

9. **(sək'ər)**
   Help; relief.
   (sək'ər) was on the way for the survivors of the
   sunken battleship.

10. **(ef'ə jē)**
    An image or a figure representing a disliked or
    hated person.
    The angry mob hanged the dictator in (ef'ə jē).

---

1. **condolence**
2. **solace**
3. **sustenance**
4. **etymology**
5. **frenetic**
6. **apparatus**
7. **dilapidated**
8. **decrepit**
9. **succor**
10. **effigy**

---

1. **(pə ren′ē əl)**
   Lasting for many years; lasting for a long time.
   Asparagus is a (pə ren′ē əl) plant; once planted,
   it sends up shoots year after year.

2. **(bī en′ē əl)**
   Lasting for two years; occurring every two years.
   Beets and carrots are (bī en′ē əl) plants; they
   produce seeds and then die in the second year.

3. **(hef′ər)**
   A young cow.
   The farmer sold the (hef′ər) for beef before it
   matured into a milk cow.

4. **(breth′rən)**
   Brothers; fellow members of a church.
   "My beloved (breth′rən)," said the minister as he
   began his sermon.

5. **(ə līn′mənt)**
   The positioning of parts into a straight line or into
   a proper order.
   A wheel (ə līn′mənt) will help make the car
   drive straight.

6. **(ə rān′mənt)**
   The act of calling a defendant before a court to
   answer a charge against him.
   At his (ə rān′mənt) the defendant entered a plea
   of "Not guilty" to the charge of burglary.

7. **(rē it′ə rāt′)**
   To say over again.
   "You may be tired of hearing the instructions, but I have to (rē it′ə rāt′) to make sure everyone understands."

8. **(mām)**
   To cripple; to injure seriously.
   Every year drunken drivers (mām) or kill thousands of people in accidents.

9. **(mā′hem)** or **(mā′əm)**
   The crime of willfully crippling or injuring a person's body.
   The kidnappers threatened to commit (mā′hem) on the hostages if the ransom wasn't paid.

10. **(poin′yənt)**
    Arousing the emotions of pity or compassion.
    The refugees told (poin′yənt) stories of their suffering from war and hunger.

---

1. **perennial**
2. **biennial**
3. **heifer**
4. **brethren**
5. **alignment**
6. **arraignment**
7. **reiterate**
8. **maim**
9. **mayhem**
10. **poignant**

---

1. (hün'tə) or (jən'tə)
   A group of leaders governing a country following a revolution.
   A military (hün'tə) of four generals took control of the government after overthrowing the king.

2. (sər vā'ləns)
   A close watch on persons under suspicion.
   The police kept the suspects under (sər vā'ləns) for days before arresting them.

3. (näk'shəs)
   Poisonous; very harmful.
   A (näk'shəs) gas leaked from a derailed tank car, posing a health hazard.

4. (äb näk'shəs) or (əb näk'shəs)
   Very unpleasant and offensive; disgusting.
   His loud talking and bad manners were so (äb näk'shəs) we left the party.

5. (flak'səd)
   Hanging loose; flabby; soft and limp.
   His muscles were (flak'səd) from lack of exercise.

6. (in ər'shə)
   The tendency of an object to stay at rest or to keep moving in the same direction.
   (in ər'shə) will help the spaceship stay on its course.

7. **(krisʹtə līzʹ)**
   To form into crystals.
   Water vapor will (krisʹtə līzʹ) into snowflakes
   when the temperature falls below freezing.

8. **(krisʹtə lən)** or **(krisʹtl ən)**
   Like crystal; clear; pure.
   The fountain splashed into the (krisʹtə lən)
   water of the pool.

9. **(avʹər əs)**
   Extreme greed.
   Because of his (avʹər əs) the man cheated his
   customers for more profit.

10. **(detʹrə menʹtl)**
    Harmful.
    Cigarette smoking is (detʹrə menʹtl) to health; it
    often causes lung cancer and heart diseases.

---

1. **junta**
2. **surveillance**
3. **noxious**
4. **obnoxious**
5. **flaccid**
6. **inertia**
7. **crystallize**
8. **crystalline**
9. **avarice**
10. **detrimental**

---

1. **(vôd′vil)** or **(vô′də vil)**
   A stage entertainment featuring songs, dances, plays, acrobatic feats, and other acts.
   The television variety show was like old-time (vôd′vil).

2. **(pech′ə lənt)**
   Showing irritation over trifles; peevish; fretful.
   The (pech′ə lənt) child wouldn't come to dinner until his mother let him have his way.

3. **(kwer′ə ləs)** or **(kwer′yə ləs)**
   Habitually complaining; fault-finding.
   Rip Van Winkle had a (kwer′ə ləs) wife who nagged him day and night.

4. **(mag′ət)**
   An insect larva that looks like a worm.
   A (mag′ət) becomes a housefly when it reaches adulthood.

5. **(im pər′vē əs)**
   Not affected by.
   This sleeping bag is (im pər′vē əs) to moisture.

6. **(präf′ə tir′ing)**
   Making unfair profits, especially in times of short supply.
   The oil companies were accused of (präf′ə tir′ing) when they raised oil prices during the fuel shortage.

7. **(di räg′ə tôr′ē)**
   Degrading; belittling.
   He would think it (di räg′ə tôr′ē) if you called
   him a sissy.

8. **(mə līn′)**
   To speak evil of or untruthfully about; to ruin the
   good name of.
   They tried to (mə līn′) an honest man by
   calling him a liar.

9. **(mə lig′nənt)**
   Very harmful; causing death.
   The patient would have died if the doctor
   hadn't removed the (mə lig′nənt) tumor.

10. **(im′pas′)** or **(im pas′)**
    A dead end; a road or a situation having no way
    out.
    We had to turn back when we came to an
    (im′pas′) on the hiking trail.

---

1. **vaudeville**
2. **petulant**
3. **querulous**
4. **maggot**
5. **impervious**
6. **profiteering**
7. **derogatory**
8. **malign**
9. **malignant**
10. **impasse**

---

1. **(tī′rənt)**
   A ruler who uses his power in a cruel and unjust way.
   The (tī′rənt) sent many people to prison for speaking out against his rule.

2. **(tir′ə nē)**
   An oppressive rule by one person who has absolute power.
   The people revolted against their king's (tir′ə nē).

3. **(tə ran′i kəl)** or **(tī ran′i kəl)**
   Cruel and unjust.
   The (tə ran′i kəl) king refused to give freedom to his people.

4. **(skərj)**
   Something that causes a great misfortune or widespread suffering.
   Famine has been a (skərj) in parts of Africa for centuries.

5. **(flā′grənt)**
   Shocking; outrageous; noticeable.
   He was expelled from the football game for his (fla′grənt) violation of the rules.

6. **(poin set′ē ə)** or **(poin set′ə)**
   A plant with small flowers surrounded by red or yellow leaves that look like flower petals.
   When I first saw a (poin set′ē ə), I thought the red leaves at the top were flowers.

7. **(kən jen′ə təl)**
   Existing from birth.
   Birthmarks are (kən jen′ə təl) blemishes on the skin.

8. **(i nāt′)** or **(in′āt)**
   Natural; inborn.
   Julie inherited an (i nāt′) love of music from her musician father.

9. **(ek strā′nē əs)** or **(ik strā′nē əs)**
   Not belonging; not essential.
   We made the water pure by filtering out sand, dust, and other (ek strā′nē əs) matter.

10. **(prə lif′ik)**
    Producing in great numbers.
    The (prə lif′ik) author wrote a book a month for five years.

---

1. **tyrant**
2. **tyranny**
3. **tyrannical**
4. **scourge**
5. **flagrant**
6. **poinsettia**
7. **congenital**
8. **innate**
9. **extraneous**
10. **prolific**

---

1. **(tə rān′)**
   A tract of land.
   That hiking trail goes over rugged (tə rān′).

2. **(tə res′trē əl)**
   Of the earth.
   The astronauts returned safely to their
   (tə res′trē əl) home.

3. **(sə les′chəl)**
   Heavenly; of the sky.
   The sun and the moon are (sə les′chəl) neighbors
   of the earth.

4. **(səb tə rā′nē ən)**
   Underground.
   Moles and chipmunks have (səb tə rā′nē ən)
   homes.

5. **(är bôr′ē əl)**
   Of trees; living in trees.
   Since monkeys and squirrels live in trees, they
   are called (är bôr′ē əl) animals.

6. **(gran′dē ōs′)**
   Large in scope; grand in style.
   The emperor had a (gran′dē ōs′) scheme to
   conquer all of Europe.

7. **(vər bā′təm)**
Word for word; in the same words.
The newspaper printed his speech (vər bā′təm).

8. **(stü′pər)** or **(styü′pər)**
A dazed or confused condition.
He was in a (stü′pər) from lack of sleep after staying up all night.

9. **(stü′pə fīd′)** or **(styü′pə fīd′)**
Astonished; dulled in the senses; stunned.
The people were (stü′pə fīd′) and grieved by the news of the king's sudden death.

10. **(lī′kən)**
A flowerless small plant that grows flat on tree trunks and rocks.
The rock had a gray patch of (lī′kən) growing on it.

---

1. **terrain**
2. **terrestrial**
3. **celestial**
4. **subterranean**
5. **arboreal**
6. **grandiose**
7. **verbatim**
8. **stupor**
9. **stupefied**
10. **lichen**

---

1. **(in dij'ə nəs)**
   Native; living naturally in a region.
   The turkey is (in dij'ə nəs) to North America.

2. **(ab'ə rij'ə nēz)**
   The earliest known inhabitants of a region.
   Before the Europeans arrived, the (ab'ə rij'ə nēz)
   of Australia lived like cavemen.

3. **(ding'ē)**
   A small rowboat.
   After their shipwreck they drifted on the ocean in
   a (ding'ē).

4. **(in'fəd əl)** or **(in'fə del')**
   A person who doesn't believe in a certain religion;
   of or relating to such persons.
   The (in'fəd əl) tribe killed all Christian
   missionaries who came to preach in their country.

5. **(shas'ē)** or **(chas'ē)**
   The frame and the parts that support the body of
   an automobile or an airplane.
   The (shas'ē) of an automobile includes the frame,
   the engine, the wheels, and the brakes.

6. **(rez'ə rek'shən)**
   The act of coming back to life; the act of rising
   from the dead.
   Spring is the time of (rez'ə rek'shən) for plants
   and flowers.

7. (es′kə pād′)
   A carefree or mischievous adventure; a prank.
   Gary was dressed like a ghost for the Halloween
   (es′kə pād′).

8. (dē′kən)
   A layman who assists a minister.
   One of his duties as (dē′kən) is to collect
   offerings during Sunday worship services.

9. (mär sü′pē əl)
   A mammal, the female of which carries its young
   in a pouch.
   The kangaroo is a large (mär sü′pē əl) of
   Australia.

10. (kō ä′lə)
    An animal of Australia that lives in trees.
    The (kō ä′lə) looks like a teddy bear.

---

1. indigenous
2. aborigines
3. dinghy
4. infidel
5. chassis
6. resurrection
7. escapade
8. deacon
9. marsupial
10. koala

---

1. **(pər'gə tôr' ē)**
    A place or a condition of temporary punishment, suffering, or misery.
    Man's work is a lifetime (pər'gə tôr'ē) if he doesn't enjoy it.

2. **(ig zôr'bə tənt)** or **(eg zôr'bə tənt)**
    Excessive.
    "I'd rather not buy it than pay that (ig zôr'bə tənt) price."

3. **(in ôrd'n ət)**
    Excessive; not within proper limits.
    He took (in ôrd'n ət) pride in his voice, but no one enjoyed listening to him sing.

4. **(bək'ə nirz')**
    Pirates.
    (bək'ə nirz') raided and robbed Spanish ships in the Caribbean.

5. **(ô'gər)**
    A hand tool for boring holes.
    The carpenter used an (ô'gər) to make a hole for the door knob.

6. **(ô'gər)**
    To foretell; to predict.
    Opinion polls (ô'gər) well for the governor who is running for reelection; they are two to one in his favor.

7. (mər'sə ner'ē)
   A soldier hired to serve in a foreign army.
   The Englishman went to fight in Africa as a
   (mər'sə ner'ē) because the pay was good and he
   loved adventure.

8. (tù bər'kyə lō'səs) or (tyù bər'kyə lō'səs)
   A contagious disease of the lungs.
   The chest X rays showed that he had
   (tù bər'kyə lō'səs).

9. (tù bər'kyə lər) or (tyù bər'kyə lər)
   Having a contagious disease of the lungs.
   The (tù bər'kyə lər) child was sent to a hospital
   in the country for treatment and rest.

10. (mir'ē əd)
    Very large in number.
    (mir'ē əd) stars adorn the night sky.

---

1. purgatory
2. exorbitant
3. inordinate
4. buccaneers
5. auger
6. augur
7. mercenary
8. tuberculosis
9. tubercular
10. myriad

---

1. **(prə pish′əs)**
   Favorable; suitable.
   New Year's Day is a (prə pish′əs) time to make resolutions.

2. **(ô spish′əs)**
   Favorable; showing signs of success.
   The good weather was an (ô spish′əs) beginning for their voyage.

3. **(ô′spə səz)** or **(ô′spə sēz′)**
   Sponsorship.
   The spelling bee was held under the (ô′spə səz) of the local newspaper.

4. **(kəm pā′trē ət)**
   A fellow countryman.
   Finding a (kəm pā′trē ət) in the distant foreign country was sheer joy for the lonesome traveler.

5. **(flam boi′ənt)**
   Showy; overly decorated; exaggerated in style.
   The clowns came on stage wearing (flam boi′ənt) costumes.

6. **(präd′i gəl)**
   Wasteful; reckless or careless in spending.
   The (präd′i gəl) son soon spent all the money his father gave him.

7. **(môr'än)**
An adult whose mental age is the same as that of a child between eight and twelve years old.
Even a (môr'än) could have passed such an easy test.

8. **(im'bə səl)** or **(im'bə sil)**
An adult whose mental age is the same as that of a child of three to seven years old; an idiot.
Even an (im'bə səl) could figure out such a simple puzzle.

9. **(ad män'ə tôr'ē)**
Giving a warning or strong advice to a person in order to correct a fault.
The judge gave the young offender an (ad män'ə tôr'ē) lecture and set him free.

10. **(bə fün')**
A clown.
He acted like a (bə fün'), making funny faces and telling ridiculous jokes.

---

1. **propitious**
2. **auspicious**
3. **auspices**
4. **compatriot**
5. **flamboyant**
6. **prodigal**
7. **moron**
8. **imbecile**
9. **admonitory**
10. **buffoon**

---

1. **(sär′kaz′əm)**
   A sneering, mocking remark; the use of sharp, bitter remarks to make fun of someone.
   When George gave the wrong answer, Martha said in (sär′kaz′əm), "How smart!"

2. **(sär dän′ik)**
   Mocking; sneering; bitterly sarcastic.
   The (sär dän′ik) laugh of the wicked witch frightened Dorothy.

3. **(mez′mə rīz′)**
   To fascinate; to charm.
   Magicians (mez′mə rīz′) people with clever tricks.

4. **(wän′tən)**
   Reckless; shameless; having no just cause.
   The killing of mourning doves is (wän′tən) cruelty.

5. **(ō′gər)**
   In fairy tales, a monster that eats people; a very cruel person.
   Only an (ō′gər) would think of robbing the poor old lady.

6. **(vō sif′ər əs)**
   Noisy; loud.
   The (vō sif′ər əs) booing of the crowd drowned out the speaker's voice.

7. **(kə lab′ə rāt′)**
   To work together.
   The two scientists decided to (kə lab′ə rāt′) on
   a research project.

8. **(kə räb′ə rāt′)**
   To support with evidence; to confirm; to prove.
   The defendant had witnesses who could
   (kə räb′ə rāt′) his testimony in court.

9. **(və lü′mə nəs)**
   Large; bulky.
   She wrote a (və lü′mə nəs) twelve-page letter to
   the editor of the *News*.

10. **(mā′sə)**
    An isolated hill with a flat top and steep sides.
    A (mā′sə) is sometimes called a table mountain
    because its flat top resembles a huge table.

---

1. sarcasm
2. sardonic
3. mesmerize
4. wanton
5. ogre
6. vociferous
7. collaborate
8. corroborate
9. voluminous
10. mesa

The Final Rounds   *131*

1. **(sat′īr)**
   A novel, a play, or an essay intended to ridicule habits, ideas, or customs of some people.
   Jonathan Swift's *Gulliver's Travels* is a (sat′īr) on man's follies.

2. **(kar′i kə chùr′)**
   A sketch that exaggerates the peculiarities of a person in an amusing or ridiculous way.
   The newspaper cartoonist drew an amusing (kar′i kə chùr′) highlighting the mayor's large nose.

3. **(bər lesk′)**
   To imitate humorously or mockingly.
   Comedians often (bər lesk′) well-known politicians.

4. **(par′ə dē)**
   A comic imitation of a serious literary or musical work; a poor imitation.
   The television show was a hilarious (par′ə dē) of Charles Dickens's *Christmas Carol*.

5. **(färs)**
   A ridiculous pretense; a ridiculous or foolish show.
   Without freedom of speech, democracy would be a (färs).

6. **(bā′ə net′)** or **(bā′ə net′)**
   A dagger that can be attached to the end of a rifle for hand-to-hand fighting.
   The guard was holding a rifle with the (bā′ə net′) fixed.

7. **(präm′ə sôr′ē)**
   Containing a promise.
   He signed a (präm′ə sôr′ē) note saying he'd pay
   the money back within a year.

8. **(kəm pat′ə bəl)**
   Able to get along together.
   Diane and her roommate were so (kəm pat′ə bəl)
   they never quarreled.

9. **(ə lak′rə tē)**
   Prompt and cheerful willingness.
   He accepted the offer with (ə lak′rə tē) because
   the pay was very good.

10. **(i lēt′) or (ā lēt′)**
    Distinguished; choice; select.
    The Baseball Hall of Fame honors the (i lēt′)
    baseball players.

---

1. satire
2. caricature
3. burlesque
4. parody
5. farce
6. bayonet
7. promissory
8. compatible
9. alacrity
10. elite

---

1. **(pə lā'shəl)**
   Of or like a palace.
   The White House is a (pə lā'shəl) mansion where
   the President lives.

2. **(bər sərk')** or **(bər zərk')**
   In a violent rage or madness.
   The crazed man went (bər sərk') with a gun and
   killed people in the street.

3. **(en skäns')** or **(in skäns')**
   To settle in a safe, comfortable, or secret place.
   After dinner he likes to (en skäns') himself in an
   armchair and read the evening paper.

4. **(ə vər'zhən)** or **(ə vər'shən)**
   Strong dislike.
   Lazy people have an (ə vər'zhən) to hard work.

5. **(lōth)**
   To have strong dislike for.
   "I (lōth) snakes; I don't even want to look at
   them."

6. **(lōth'səm)** or **(loth'səm)**
   Disgusting; offensive.
   The rotten fish had a (lōth'səm) smell.

7. **(sī'məl tā'nē əs)**
Happening at the same time.
In a (sī'məl tā'nē əs) attack, airplanes bombed
and artillery shelled the fortress.

8. **(em pir'i kəl)**
Based on observation or experience; experimental.
He did an (em pir'i kəl) study to show that his
theory was correct.

9. **(mā'trē ärk')**
A woman who rules a family or a tribe.
After Mary's grandfather passed away, her
grandmother became the (mā'trē ärk') of her
large family.

10. **(pā'trē ärk')**
The father and ruler of a family or a tribe.
The old (pā'trē ärk') and his sons came to live
with Joseph in Egypt.

---

1. palatial
2. berserk
3. ensconce
4. aversion
5. loathe
6. loathsome
7. simultaneous
8. empirical
9. matriarch
10. patriarch

---

1. **(plā′jə riz′əm)**
   The act of copying another's ideas or writings as one's own.
   You may be accused of (plā′jə riz′əm) if you don't tell whose quotations you're using.

2. **(hə rang′)**
   A long, noisy speech.
   After losing the game, we sat for hours listening to our coach's (hə rang′).

3. **(tī rād′)** or **(tī′rād′)**
   A long, angry, or scolding speech.
   Rip Van Winkle's wife screamed a (tī rād′) of complaints at him.

4. **(pərl)**
   A gentle murmuring sound of a rippling stream.
   The (pərl) of the brook lulled the campers to sleep.

5. **(näk tər′nəl)**
   Active at night; of the night.
   (näk tər′nəl) animals, like owls and raccoons, sleep during the day and feed at night.

6. **(ə nak′rə niz′əm)**
   A person or a thing that is out of its proper historical time.
   A picture of George Washington riding in an automobile would be an (ə nak′rə niz′əm).

---

7. **(kwi zēn′)**
   The style of preparing food.
   This restaurant is known for its fine (kwi zēn′)
   and friendly service.

8. **(kyü′lə ner′ē) or (kəl′ə ner′ē)**
   Of or related to cooking or to the kitchen.
   Her dinner was a (kyü′lə ner′ē) masterpiece that
   pleased all the guests.

9. **(ther′ə pyü′tik)**
   Serving to heal or cure; beneficial.
   Swimming every day after her knee operation
   had a (ther′ə pyü′tik) effect.

10. **(nā′dər)**
    The lowest point; the time of great misfortune.
    Tom was at the (nā′dər) of despair when he
    couldn't find a way out of the cave.

---

1. **plagiarism**
2. **harangue**
3. **tirade**
4. **purl**
5. **nocturnal**
6. **anachronism**
7. **cuisine**
8. **culinary**
9. **therapeutic**
10. **nadir**

---

1. **(skrü′pəl)**
   To hesitate about doing something that isn't right.
   That salesman didn't (skrü′pəl) to tell lies to make money.

2. **(skrü′pyə ləs)**
   Strict in doing what is right.
   The judge was (skrü′pyə ləs) in holding a fair trial.

3. **(mə tik′yə ləs)**
   Very careful with details.
   He examined the laboratory sample with (mə tik′yə ləs) care.

4. **(kər′sər ē)**
   Hasty; casual; not thorough.
   He gave the morning paper a (kər′sər ē) glance while eating breakfast.

5. **(ə sim′ə lāt′)**
   To absorb and adopt as one's own.
   America was able to (ə sim′ə lāt′) immigrants from all parts of the world.

6. **(ən wôn′təd), (ən wōn′təd),** or **(ən wən′təd)**
   Unusual; not customary.
   His (ən wôn′təd) behavior puzzled his friends.

7. (ôrd'nəns)
   Military supplies including guns and ammunition;
   cannon or artillery.
   The army needs well-trained soldiers and proper
   (ôrd'nəns) to win the war.

8. (ôrd'n əns) or (ôrd'nəns)
   A local law.
   A city (ôrd'n əns) forbids parking in front of
   fire hydrants.

9. (in grā'shē āt')
   To bring oneself into another's favor.
   He tried to (in grā'shē āt') himself with his
   boss by flattery.

10. (sü'pər sil'ē əs)
    Haughty and proud; contemptuous.
    The champion cast a (sü'pər sil'ē əs) glance at
    his opponent.

---

1. scruple
2. scrupulous
3. meticulous
4. cursory
5. assimilate
6. unwonted
7. ordnance
8. ordinance
9. ingratiate
10. supercilious

---

1. (kän'də min'ē əm)
   An apartment building in which each apartment is owned by the people who live in it; an apartment in such a building.
   The five families who live in that (kän'də min'ē əm) share the swimming pool and the tennis courts.

2. (flip'ənt lē)
   Characterized by lack of respect or seriousness.
   He joked (flip'ənt lē) when the teacher asked him a serious question.

3. (friv'ə ləs)
   Silly; not serious; unworthy of attention.
   The committee wasted half an hour listening to her (friv'ə ləs) objections to the proposal.

4. (nän'shə läns') or (nän'shə ləns)
   Cool indifference; casualness; unconcern.
   With seeming (nän'shə läns'), he kept on speaking to the booing crowd.

5. (al'bə trôs') or (al'bə träs')
   A large seabird that can fly a long distance.
   The (al'bə trôs') is the largest seabird; its wings often spread more than ten feet.

6. (i rev'ə kə bəl)
   Not to be changed or withdrawn.
   His decision was (i rev'ə kə bəl); no one could make him change his mind.

7. (man'ə kyùr'əst)
   A person whose job is cleaning, trimming, and
   polishing the fingernails.
   While getting a haircut in the beauty shop, she
   had a (man'ə kyùr'əst) trim her fingernails.

8. (ser'ə nād')
   To sing or play a light, sentimental song for one's
   sweetheart.
   In Shakespeare's *Romeo and Juliet*, Romeo
   comes in the evening to (ser'ə nād') Juliet with
   his melodious voice.

9. (är thrī'təs)
   A swelling, pain, and stiffness in joints of the
   body.
   (är thrī'təs) in her fingers prevented
   Grandmother from doing needlework.

10. (rü'mə tiz'əm)
    A disease of the muscles and the joints, causing
    stiffness and pain.
    Because of (rü'mə tiz'əm) she couldn't easily go
    up and down stairs.

---

1. condominium
2. flippantly
3. frivolous
4. nonchalance
5. albatross
6. irrevocable
7. manicurist
8. serenade
9. arthritis
10. rheumatism

---

1. **(sər′kət)**
   A path over which an electric current flows.
   Electricity will flow through the (sər′kət) when
   you turn on the switch.

2. **(sər kyü′ə təs)**
   Roundabout; not direct.
   Bob took a (sər kyü′ə təs) route home on his
   bicycle to avoid steep hills.

3. **(rəf′ē ən)**
   A rough, brutal, or cruel person.
   The (rəf′ē ən) attacked them, then stole their
   money.

4. **(ed′ə fəs)**
   A large, impressive building.
   The Capitol is an (ed′ə fəs) of stone housing
   both the Senate and the House of
   Representatives.

5. **(i rep′ər ə bəl)**
   Incapable of being repaired.
   The accident caused (i rep′ər ə bəl) damage to
   the car.

6. **(in kôr′ə jə bəl)** or **(in kär′ə jə bəl)**
   Bad beyond all hopes of being corrected or
   reformed.
   The (in kôr′ə jə bəl) youth spent most of his life
   in reformatories.

---

7. **(flə ming′gō)**
A tropical wading bird having pink feathers.
The (flə ming′gō) stood still, resting on one leg.

8. **(ō bā′səns)** or **(ō bē′səns)**
A gesture expressing respect or submission, such as
a bow.
The knights made (ō bā′səns) to the queen as
she entered the room.

9. **(rek′wə zət)**
Something that cannot be done without; an
essential requirement.
A good speaking voice is a (rek′wə zət) for a
radio announcer.

10. **(dek′strəs)** or **(dek′stər əs)**
Skillful.
You must be (dek′strəs) with your hands to
perform magicians' tricks.

---

1. **circuit**
2. **circuitous**
3. **ruffian**
4. **edifice**
5. **irreparable**
6. **incorrigible**
7. **flamingo**
8. **obeisance**
9. **requisite**
10. **dexterous** or **dextrous**

---

1. **(kə tas′trə fē)**
   A sudden, severe disaster or misfortune.
   (kə tas′trə fē) struck the town when the tornado
   ripped through its main streets.

2. **(di bä′kəl)** or **(di bak′əl)**
   A sudden disaster or defeat; a sudden and complete
   downfall.
   Napoleon's invasion into Russia ended in a
   (di bä′kəl) which cost him half a million soldiers.

3. **(fē as′kō)**
   A complete and often ridiculous failure.
   The boxing match ended in a (fē as′kō) for the
   defending champion, who was knocked out in the
   second round.

4. **(kat′ə kliz′mik)**
   Extremely sudden and violent; causing a violent
   change; disastrous.
   The eruption of Mount Vesuvius brought
   (kat′ə kliz′mik) ruin on Pompeii, burying the
   entire city under piles of ashes.

5. **(häl′ə kôst′)** or **(hō′lə kôst′)**
   A complete or widespread destruction and loss of
   life, especially by fire.
   The atomic (häl′ə kôst′) turned the city of
   Hiroshima into ashes.

6. **(i ras′ə bəl)** or **(ī ras′ə bəl)**
   Easily angered.
   The (i ras′ə bəl) old man often quarreled with
   his neighbors.

7. (rel′ə gāt′)

To send or assign to a lower position.
"If you don't play well on the varsity team, the coach will (rel′ə gāt′) you to junior varsity."

8. (bi rēvd′)

Having lost a loved person by death.
The (bi rēvd′) citizens mourned the death of their President.

9. (steth′ə skōp′)

A doctor's instrument for listening to heartbeats and other sounds produced in the body.
The doctor listened to my heart beat through his (steth′ə skōp′).

10. (mek′ə)

A place visited by many people.
The playground was a (mek′ə) for neighborhood children.

---

1. catastrophe
2. debacle
3. fiasco
4. cataclysmic
5. holocaust
6. irascible
7. relegate
8. bereaved
9. stethoscope
10. mecca

---

1. **(man′də lin′)** or **(man′də lin′)**
   A stringed musical instrument with a sound box
   shaped like a pear.
   Jerry strummed his (man′də lin′) and began to
   sing.

2. **(thrôl)**
   A slave.
   The man was a (thrôl) to alcohol from habitual
   drinking.

3. **(i mak′yə lət)**
   Spotlessly clean; flawless.
   The nurses were dressed in (i mak′yə lət) white
   uniforms.

4. **(im pek′ə bəl)**
   Faultless; flawless.
   His table manners are (im pek′ə bəl).

5. **(dī′ə bē′təs)** or **(dī′ə bē′tēz)**
   A disease marked by too much sugar in the blood
   and the urine.
   He shouldn't eat candies or other sweets because
   he has (dī′ə bē′təs).

6. **(met′ə môr′fə səs)**
   Changes in shape and function some animals go
   through during their life cycles.
   Caterpillars become butterflies by
   (met′ə môr′fə səs).

7. (er′ā tər) or (ar′ā tər)
A device used for mixing air into something.
The (er′ā tər) in the aquarium pumps air into
the water to provide oxygen for the fish.

8. (er′ə sôl′), (er′ə säl′), (ar′ə sôl′), or (ar′ə säl′)
A mass of fine liquid particles kept under pressure
in a can.
Insect sprays are often sold in (er′ə sôl′) cans.

9. (kän′sə krāt′)
To dedicate for a worthy cause.
The monks made a sacred vow to (kän′sə krāt′)
their lives to the church.

10. (stôl′wərt)
Stout; firm and reliable.
The United States was a (stôl′wərt) ally of
England in World War II.

---

1. mandolin
2. thrall
3. immaculate
4. impeccable
5. diabetes
6. metamorphosis
7. aerator
8. aerosol
9. consecrate
10. stalwart

---

1. **(bûr)**
   A person with clumsy, rude manners.
   "Don't be a (bûr); act like a gentleman."

2. **(ən küth′)**
   Awkward; crude.
   His (ən küth′) table manners annoyed his hostess.

3. **(gōsh)**
   Lacking social grace; awkward.
   His (gōsh) remarks embarrassed the hostess.

4. **(ər bān′)**
   Well-mannered; poised and courteous.
   She was (ər bān′) and friendly—a charming hostess.

5. **(swäv)**
   Smoothly polite; gracious; well-mannered.
   The ambassador was (swäv) and courteous in answering the reporter's questions.

6. **(ab′ses)**
   A mass of pus in some part of the body.
   Severe tooth decay can cause an (ab′ses).

7. (mə träp′ə ləs)
A large and important city.
Atlanta is now a (mə träp′ə ləs) of the South,
but was once a small railroad town.

8. (prō zā′ik)
Commonplace; ordinary; unimaginative.
(prō zā′ik) jokes are boring.

9. (än säm′bəl)
A group of musicians performing together.
Steve plays violin in the string (än säm′bəl).

10. (hip′ə pät′ə məs)
A large animal that lives in or near the rivers of
Africa.
The (hip′ə pät′ə məs) can stay under water for
hours by keeping its nostrils above the surface.

---

1. boor
2. uncouth
3. gauche
4. urbane
5. suave
6. abscess
7. metropolis
8. prosaic
9. ensemble
10. hippopotamus

---

1. **(ri splen′dənt)**
   Shining brilliantly.
   The jeweler's showcase was (ri splen′dənt) with
   diamonds.

2. **(ō pāk′)**
   Not letting light through; not transparent.
   He painted the windowpane black to make it
   (ō pāk′).

3. **(tər′bəd)**
   Muddy.
   The storm filled the creek with (tər′bəd) water.

4. **(tər′jəd)**
   Swollen; inflated.
   His sprained ankle was red and (tər′jəd).

5. **(äs′tən tā′shəs)**
   Showy; done to impress others.
   Proud of his wealth, the millionaire lived in an
   (äs′tən tā′shəs) mansion.

6. **(zef′ər)**
   A gentle breeze.
   A (zef′ər) rustled through the pine leaves.

---

7. **(ə klī′mət)** or **(ak′lə māt′)**
To become accustomed to a new environment.
It was difficult for Susan to (ə klī′mət) herself
to winters in Alaska after moving from Florida.

8. **(ak′lə mā′shən)**
An oral vote of approval without a ballot; an
enthusiastic applause.
The members of the football team elected their
captain by (ak′lə mā′shən).

9. **(kən gläm′ər ət)**
A company doing business in many different fields.
His company has grown into a huge
(kən gläm′ər ət) that makes cars, chemicals, and
appliances.

10. **(rī näs′ər əs)**
A large thick-skinned animal having one or two
horns rising from its snout.
The (rī näs′ər əs) is almost as large as the
hippopotamus.

---

1. resplendent
2. opaque
3. turbid
4. turgid
5. ostentatious
6. zephyr
7. acclimate
8. acclamation
9. conglomerate
10. rhinoceros

---

1. **(bas´chən)**
   A part of a fortification that sticks out from the main body; a fortified position for defense.
   The defenders fired guns from behind the (bas´chən) of the fortress wall.

2. **(bùl´wərk)**
   A wall built for defense; something that defends or protects.
   The tall cliff served as a (bùl´wərk) protecting the fortress from attackers.

3. **(ak´wē es´)**
   To agree without protest; to accept reluctantly.
   Tom decided to (ak´wē es´) in the plan, since everyone else liked it.

4. **(säd´n)**
   Soaked through.
   His clothes and shoes were (säd´n) after he walked home in the rain.

5. **(im pēd´)**
   To hinder; to hold back.
   The shortage of scientists may (im pēd´) our progress in research.

6. **(im ped´ə mənt)**
   An obstruction; something that holds back; a defect.
   Not knowing how to speak English can be a serious (im ped´ə mənt) to an immigrant.

7. (môr′ə tôr′ē əm) or (mär′ə tôr′ē əm)
A delay of action; a temporary ban.
The government ordered a (môr′ə tôr′ē əm) on
building nuclear plants until safe operation could
be assured.

8. (yü′zhər ē)
The practice of lending money at an unlawfully
high rate.
The (yü′zhər ē) law forbade anyone from
charging more than eighteen percent interest.

9. (yü′zhər ər)
A person who lends money at an unlawfully high
interest rate.
The pawnbroker, a (yü′zhər ər), charged more
than double the interest allowed by law.

10. (yü sər′pər)
One who takes over the power or the position of
another without legal right.
While the king was still a child, his wicked
uncle became a (yü sər′pər) of the royal powers.

---

1. bastion
2. bulwark
3. acquiesce
4. sodden
5. impede
6. impediment
7. moratorium
8. usury
9. usurer
10. usurper

---

1. **(ô das′ə tē)**
   Courage in taking risks; reckless boldness.
   The explorer had the (ô das′ə tē) to travel alone
   by sled to the North Pole.

2. **(tə mer′ə tē)**
   Reckless or foolish boldness.
   No one had the (tə mer′ə tē) to argue with the
   angry king.

3. **(i frən′tər ē)**
   Shameless boldness.
   The reporter had the (i frən′tər ē) to insult the
   mayor during a news conference.

4. **(dif′ə dənt)**
   Timid; lacking confidence.
   He spoke with a low, (dif′ə dənt) voice that no
   one in the back of the room could hear.

5. **(az′mə)**
   A disease that causes coughing, wheezing, and
   difficulty in breathing.
   He couldn't run without coughing because he had
   (az′mə).

6. **(byù räk′rə sē)**
   A government by many officials who tend to follow
   rigid rules.
   His visa application had to go through a maze of
   (byù räk′rə sē) before it was approved.

7. **(tich´ə lər)**
   Having the title of an office without the duties or the powers.
   The king became only a (tich´ə lər) ruler after his power was given to the newly-elected president.

8. **(äs´ə lā´shən)**
   The act of swinging back and forth between two points.
   That clock pendulum makes one (äs´ə lā´shən) every second.

9. **(vas´ə lāt´)**
   To waver in mind; to hesitate.
   "Make up your mind and stick to your decision; don't (vas´ə lāt´)."

10. **(ən´jə lā´shən) or (ən´dyə lā´shən)**
    A rhythmic rising and falling movement.
    The gust of wind caused an (ən´jə lā´shən) in the wheat field.

---

1. **audacity**
2. **temerity**
3. **effrontery**
4. **diffident**
5. **asthma**
6. **bureaucracy**
7. **titular**
8. **oscillation**
9. **vacillate**
10. **undulation**

---

1. (mäl′ə fī′)
   To soothe in temper; to calm.
   "To (mäl′ə fī′) her anger, I apologized."

2. (plā′kāt) or (plak′āt)
   To soothe the anger of.
   To (plā′kāt) his angry customer, the store owner
   gave him a new bicycle in exchange.

3. (ə lē′vē āt′)
   To relieve; to lessen.
   Taking aspirin helped (ə lē′vē āt′) his headache.

4. (ə swāj′)
   To ease; to relieve.
   Nothing could (ə swāj′) his pain.

5. (sə rē′brəl) or (ser′ə brəl)
   Of the brain.
   Thinking is a (sə rē′brəl) activity.

6. (gal′və nīzd′)
   a. Plated with zinc.
      The wire in the fence has been (gal′və nīzd′) so
      it won't rust.
   b. Stirred up as if by an electric shock.
      The coach's pep talk (gal′və nīzd′) the team into
      playing a winning game.

7. (ri nig′), (ri neg′), or (ri nēg′)
   To go back on a promise.
   His words are as good as gold; he won't (ri nig′).

8. (ren′ə gād′)
   A person who deserts his religion or political party
   to join the other side.
   The (ren′ə gād′) has been shunned by his
   former friends since he switched political parties.

9. (sə nôr′əs) or (sän′ər əs)
   Full, deep, and loud in sound; richly resonant.
   The speaker's (sə nôr′əs) voice rang through the
   auditorium.

10. (bel′frē)
    A bell tower.
    Bells rang in the church (bel′frē).

---

1. mollify
2. placate
3. alleviate
4. assuage
5. cerebral
6. galvanized
7. renege
8. renegade
9. sonorous
10. belfry

---

1. **(gam′ət)**
   The entire range.
   This novel covers the (gam′ət) of emotions from sorrow to joy.

2. **(sôr′sər ər)**
   A person who practices magic with the supposed aid of evil spirits.
   Trying to cure a sick child, the (sôr′sər ər) performed mysterious rites.

3. **(pər nish′əs)**
   Very destructive or harmful.
   Drug addiction is a (pər nish′əs) habit that often causes death.

4. **(i näk′yü əs)**
   Harmless; inoffensive.
   Jeff said it as an (i näk′yü əs) joke, but Betsy took it as an insult.

5. **(bläk)**
   A group of people or nations joined temporarily for common interests.
   If Representatives and Senators work together to pass laws benefiting farmers, they can be called a farm (bläk).

6. **(an′thrə poid′)**
   Resembling man; manlike.
   (an′thrə poid′) apes catch colds just like humans.

7. **(kar′ə län′)** or **(kar′ə lən)**

A set of bells hung in a tower and sounded by hammers from a keyboard.

The (kar′ə län′) in the church belfry chimed hymns.

8. **(kar′ē ən)**

Decaying flesh of a dead animal.

Vultures ate the (kar′ē ən) and left only the bones.

9. **(ef′ə kā′shəs)**

Able to produce a desired result.

Aspirin is (ef′ə kā′shəs) in treating minor headaches.

10. **(pā′thäs)**

A feeling of sadness or pity.

His farewell speech gave the audience a moment of (pā′thäs).

---

1. **gamut**
2. **sorcerer**
3. **pernicious**
4. **innocuous**
5. **bloc**
6. **anthropoid**
7. **carillon**
8. **carrion**
9. **efficacious**
10. **pathos**

---

1. **(stō′ik)**
   A person who seems indifferent to pain or pleasure;
   seemingly indifferent to pain or pleasure.
   The patient bore pain with (stō′ik) courage.

2. **(stäl′əd)**
   Showing little emotion; not easily excited.
   The (stäl′əd) coach neither smiled nor frowned as
   he watched his team play.

3. **(met′ə fôr′)** or **(met′ə fər)**
   A figure of speech in which something is described
   as something else to suggest a likeness between the
   two things.
   "He has a computer brain" is a (met′ə fôr′)
   meaning his brain works like a computer.

4. **(sim′ə lē)**
   A figure of speech beginning with *as* or *like* to
   compare two unlike things.
   "His brain works like a computer" is a (sim′ə lē).

5. **(ə nal′ə gəs)**
   Similar in some ways; comparable.
   The function of the heart is (ə nal′ə gəs) to that
   of a pump.

6. **(bā′ləf)**
   A sheriff's deputy who delivers messages or
   preserves order in a courtroom.
   A (bā′ləf) asked everyone to stand when the
   judge entered the courtroom.

7. **(kə läs'əl)**
Huge; enormous.
The pyramids of Egypt are (kə läs'əl) structures towering above the desert.

8. **(hər'kyə lē'ən)** or **(hər'kyü'lē ən)**
Requiring great effort.
Feeding and supplying the large army was a (hər'kyə lē'ən) task.

9. **(sab'ə täzh')**
The destruction of property by enemy agents in war or by workers in a labor dispute.
The striking workers' (sab'ə täzh') caused the gas tank to blow up at the factory.

10. **(dal mā'shən)**
A dog having a smooth white coat with small black spots.
Our (dal mā'shən) is a good watchdog.

---

1. stoic
2. stolid
3. metaphor
4. simile
5. analogous
6. bailiff
7. colossal
8. herculean
9. sabotage
10. dalmatian

---

1. (sü′pər sēd′)
   To replace; to take the place of.
   The prices in the new catalog will (sü′pər sēd′)
   the old ones.

2. (in′tər sēd′)
   To plead for another; to mediate in dispute.
   The governor asked the President to (in′tər sēd′)
   with the coal miners' union to end their long
   strike.

3. (in′tər vēn′)
   To come between; to come in or between to help
   settle a dispute.
   The governor was asked to (in′tər vēn′) in the
   labor dispute to help end it quickly.

4. (av′ə kä′dō) or (ä′və kä′dō)
   A pear-shaped tropical fruit with a dark green skin
   and a large, hard pit.
   She sliced an (av′ə kä′dō) to put in the salad.

5. (klē shā′)
   A phrase or an expression that has lost its
   freshness through overuse.
   The phrase "hungry as a bear" is now a (klē shā′).

6. (rep′ər twär′)
   A list of plays or songs that an actor, a musician,
   or a theatrical company has learned to perform or
   sing.
   She will sing any song you like from her large
   (rep′ər twär′) of popular songs.

7. (ak′ə lād′)
Praise; award; honor.
The quarterback received the highest (ak′ə lād′)
in college football, the Heisman Trophy.

8. (kyü′däs′), (kü′däs′), (kyü′dōs′), or (kü′dōs′)
Praise; acclaim.
The poet received many (kyü′däs′), including
honorary doctorates from several universities.

9. (der′ə lik′shən)
A failure in duty; a willful neglect of one's duty.
Because of the policeman's (der′ə lik′shən), the
suspect escaped from jail.

10. (gaz′ə tir′)
A geographical dictionary.
I looked in the (gaz′ə tir′) to find out the
population of that town.

---

1. supersede
2. intercede
3. intervene
4. avocado
5. cliché
6. repertoire
7. accolade
8. kudos
9. dereliction
10. gazetteer

---

1. **(pri kar′ē əs)** or **(pri ker′ē əs)**
   Risky; dangerous; insecure.
   The mountain climber held on to a (pri kar′ē əs)
   foothold on the icy ledge of the cliff.

2. **(ek′sə dəs)**
   A departure of a large number of people.
   Many urban families joined the (ek′sə dəs) to the
   suburbs.

3. **(in klem′ənt)**
   Stormy; rough.
   In case of (in klem′ənt) weather we'll have our
   picnic in the lodge.

4. **(in′krə mənt)**
   An increase; an added amount.
   His boss promised him an (in′krə mənt) of ten
   dollars in his pay every four months.

5. **(fə nes′)**
   Delicate skill; artfulness.
   He plays hockey with great (fə nes′).

6. **(ak′ə līt′)**
   An assistant to a priest.
   An (ak′ə līt′) lighted candles at the altar while
   the choir sang a hymn.

7. **(kän'di send')**
To come down graciously to the level of one's inferiors; to humble oneself.
The king wouldn't (kän'di send') to talk with the peasants.

8. **(dān)**
To lower oneself graciously or kindly; to think it fitting to one's dignity.
He was so haughty he didn't (dān) to answer my letter.

9. **(sak'rə mənt)**
Any of several sacred ceremonies of the Christian church.
Baptism is a (sak'rə mənt) in which a person is dipped in or sprinkled with water as a sign of having his or her sins cleansed.

10. **(mat'rə mō'nē)**
Marriage; the ceremony of marriage.
The couple were joined in (mat'rə mō'nē) at a large church wedding.

---

1. precarious
2. exodus
3. inclement
4. increment
5. finesse
6. acolyte
7. condescend
8. deign
9. sacrament
10. matrimony

1. **(mə ling′gər ər)**
   A person who pretends to be ill to avoid doing work.
   The (mə ling′gər ər) limped along, acting as if he had injured his knee and couldn't walk.

2. **(fər′mə mənt)**
   The sky.
   Millions of stars adorn the (fər′mə mənt).

3. **(hip′ə krit)**
   A person who pretends to be other than what he or she really is in character, feelings, or beliefs.
   "I'd be a (hip′ə krit) if I didn't live by what I preach to others."

4. **(hi päk′rə sē)**
   The act or practice of pretending to be what one is not in character, feelings, or beliefs.
   "It would be (hi päk′rə sē) for me to tell others to save energy while I waste it."

5. **(hī päth′ə səs)**
   An assumption proposed as a basis to show that something is true; a theory.
   His (hī päth′ə səs) was proven correct by the experiment.

6. **(fresh′ət)**
   A sudden overflowing of a stream, caused by rain or melting snow.
   A muddy (fresh′ət) from thawing snow and spring rains made the road impassable.

7. **(aj′əngkt)**
Something added or attached to another in a less important capacity.
The souvenir shop is an (aj′əngkt) of the museum.

8. **(aj′ə tənt)**
An army officer assisting the commanding officer.
The (aj′ə tənt) answered the letter for the general.

9. **(i kwiv′ə kāt′)**
To speak with double meaning in order to mislead or avoid a direct answer.
"Don't (i kwiv′ə kāt′); say yes or no."

10. **(bräk′ə lē)**
A plant whose green stalks and flower buds are eaten as a vegetable.
She boiled (bräk′ə lē) and served it with a cheese sauce.

---

1. **malingerer**
2. **firmament**
3. **hypocrite**
4. **hypocrisy**
5. **hypothesis**
6. **freshet**
7. **adjunct**
8. **adjutant**
9. **equivocate**
10. **broccoli** or **brocoli**

---

1. **(in′ən dāt′)**
   To overflow; to flood.
   If the dam breaks, water will (in′ən dāt′) the valley.

2. **(spē′shəs)**
   Seemingly attractive, true, or sincere, but actually not so; deceptive.
   The police saw through the (spē′shəs) alibi offered by the suspect and arrested him.

3. **(pär′lā)** or **(pär′lē)**
   To manage (money, talent, or other assets) to gain great wealth or success.
   He was able to (pär′lā) his small investment into a fortune.

4. **(pär′lē)**
   A conference with an opponent or with an enemy.
   At the peace (pär′lē), both sides agreed to exchange prisoners of war.

5. **(hem′ər ij)** or **(hem′rij)**
   A heavy bleeding.
   The soldier died from a (hem′ər ij) soon after he was wounded by a bullet.

6. **(ves′tə byül′)**
   A small entrance hall between the outer door and the interior of a building.
   After entering the front door, he left his hat and coat in the (ves′tə byül′).

---

7. **(klar voi'əns)** or **(kler voi'əns)**
   The ability, claimed by some persons, to know or
   see things that are out of the range of human
   senses.
   He knew by (klar voi'əns) when and where the
   accident would happen.

8. **(ə kəlt')** or **(äk'əlt)**
   Mysterious; beyond ordinary human knowledge;
   supernatural.
   Some people believe in (ə kəlt') arts like
   fortune-telling and astrology.

9. **(far'ō), (fer'ō),** or **(fā'rō)**
   A ruler of ancient Egypt.
   The (far'ō) had his people build the great
   pyramids of Egypt.

10. **(ed'ə fī')**
    To instruct and enlighten the mind.
    The stories in *Aesop's Fables* (ed'ə fī') and
    amuse readers.

---

1. **inundate**
2. **specious**
3. **parlay**
4. **parley**
5. **hemorrhage**
6. **vestibule**
7. **clairvoyance**
8. **occult**
9. **pharaoh**
10. **edify**

---

1. (kən sil'ē ə tôr'ē)
   Tending to win over or make friendly.
   As a (kən sil'ē ə tôr'ē) gesture, Jeff apologized
   for having started the quarrel.

2. (rek'ən sil'ē ā'shən)
   The act of restoring friendly relations.
   They never quarreled after their
   (rek'ən sil'ē ā'shən).

3. (i rek'ən sī'lə bəl) or (i rek'ən sī'lə bəl)
   Incapable of being resolved or brought into
   agreement.
   Their (i rek'ən sī'lə bəl) differences eventually led
   to a civil war.

4. (ā'lē ə nāt') or (āl'yə nāt')
   To lose friendship; to make someone become
   unfriendly.
   You will (ā'lē ə nāt') your friends if you criticize
   them too much.

5. (in āl'yə nə bəl) or (in ā'lē ə nə bəl)
   Not to be taken away.
   Freedom of speech is an (in āl'yə nə bəl) right
   of all Americans, guaranteed by our Constitution.

6. (bā'bəl) or (bab'əl)
   A confusion of voices.
   The (bā'bəl) of the crowd filled the auditorium
   during intermission.

7. **(kyü)**
To form a waiting line; to stand in a line.
Since many people were waiting, we had to
(kyü) up to get on the bus.

8. **(azh'ər)**
Sky-blue; the clear blue color of the cloudless sky.
Not a cloud could be found in the (azh'ər) sky.

9. **(rev'ə lē)**
A bugle call or a drumbeat early in the morning
to wake up soldiers or sailors for the day's duty.
The bugle sounded (rev'ə lē) at 6:00 a.m. to get
the soldiers up for their day's duties.

10. **(kô'li flou'ər)** or **(käl'i flou'ər)**
A plant related to the cabbage and broccoli,
having a white, round head.
(kô'li flou'ər) is eaten like broccoli.

---

1. **conciliatory**
2. **reconciliation**
3. **irreconcilable**
4. **alienate**
5. **inalienable**
6. **babel**
7. **queue**
8. **azure**
9. **reveille**
10. **cauliflower**

The Final Rounds

1. **(des′əl tôr′ē)**
   Aimless; disconnected; shifting around.
   In a (des′əl tôr′ē) way they talked about several topics.

2. **(ə sij′ü əs)**
   Diligent; industrious.
   Learning to speak a foreign language requires long, (ə sij′ü əs) study.

3. **(ep′ə lôg′) or (ep′ə läg′)**
   A concluding section of a play or a story.
   The television program ended with an (ep′ə lôg′) explaining what happened to the bank robbers after they were arrested.

4. **(ep′ə taf′)**
   An inscription on a tombstone in memory of a dead person.
   The (ep′ə taf′) on the tombstone read, "She has gone to rest in her heavenly abode."

5. **(i pit′ə mē)**
   A person or a thing that symbolizes or typifies something.
   Always cheerful and never sick, Aunt Sue was the (i pit′ə mē) of health.

6. **(ri dən′dənt)**
   Exceeding what is needed; needlessly repetitive; wordy.
   The word *hot* is (ri dən′dənt) in *hot-water heater*.

7. **(ik splis′ət)** or **(ek splis′ət)**
Precise; clear.
The doctor gave her (ik splis′ət) instructions on
how to take the medicine.

8. **(im plis′ət)**
Suggested or understood, but not plainly stated.
The mayor said he hadn't decided yet, but his
intention to run for reelection was (im plis′ət)
in his speech.

9. **(klēk)** or **(klik)**
A small exclusive group of close friends or
associates.
The chairman and his (klēk) dominated the
committee.

10. **(rev′ər ē)**
A daydream.
Jack was lost in (rev′ər ē) and didn't hear what
the teacher said.

---

1. **desultory**
2. **assiduous**
3. **epilogue**
4. **epitaph**
5. **epitome**
6. **redundant**
7. **explicit**
8. **implicit**
9. **clique**
10. **reverie** or **revery**

---

1. **(ri sind′)**
   To make officially void; to annul.
   The people asked the king to (ri sind′) the unfair tax law.

2. **(ab′rə gāt′)**
   To abolish; to annul.
   Congress voted to (ab′rə gāt′) the unpopular law.

3. **(prī mē′vəl)**
   Of the earliest age of the world; primitive.
   Giant trees grew in the (prī mē′vəl) forest untouched by man.

4. **(des′tə tüt′)** or **(des′tə tyüt′)**
   Very poor.
   The (des′tə tüt′) families relied on welfare money for their food and rent.

5. **(ō blēk′)** or **(ə blēk′)**
   Slanting; sloping; neither perpendicular nor parallel.
   That street branches at an (ō blēk′) angle, forming a fork.

6. **(ə nī′ə lāt′)**
   To destroy completely.
   This bomb is so powerful that it can (ə nī′ə lāt′) an entire city.

7. (än′tù räzh′)

   A group of associates or attendants of an important person.

   The President traveled with a large (än′tù räzh′) of aides and reporters.

9. (shēk)

   Stylish; fashionable.

   The actress looked glamorous in her (shēk) dress.

8. (ret′n ü′) or (ret′n yü′)

   A group of attendants or servants of an important person.

   The king and his (ret′n ü′) of fifty men left the palace for a long journey.

10. (hə bich′ü ā′) or (hə bich′ü ā′)

    A person who goes often to a place.

    He is a (hə bich′ü ā′) of that French restaurant; he usually goes there for dinner on weekends.

---

1. rescind
2. abrogate
3. primeval
4. destitute
5. oblique
6. annihilate
7. entourage
8. retinue
9. chic
10. habitué

---

1. **(rāth)**
    A ghost; a ghostly appearance of a person seen just before or just after death.
    The (rāth) stood silently at the door, then disappeared like smoke.

2. **(ap′ə rish′ən)**
    A strange sight; a ghost.
    The (ap′ə rish′ən) seemed to float through the locked door.

3. **(kan tang′kər əs)**
    Ill-tempered; quarrelsome.
    The (kan tang′kər əs) old man wouldn't let the children walk through his yard.

4. **(sə blīm′)**
    Noble; uplifting; majestic; inspiring awe.
    She likes all music, from the ordinary to the (sə blīm′).

5. **(dī′ə rē′ə)**
    A frequent and loose discharge of the bowels.
    His stomachache and (dī′ə rē′ə) caused him many trips to the bathroom.

6. **(i fem′ər əl)**
    Lasting a very short time.
    The mayfly is an (i fem′ər əl) insect; it lives only a few hours after reaching the adult stage.

---

7. **(rap′sə dē)**

   a. A highly emotional or enthusiastic expression.
   The announcer went into a (rap′sə dē) over the team's winning touchdown.

   b. In music, an instrumental composition irregular in form, often based on folk tunes.
   Many concert pianists enjoy playing Gershwin's "(rap′sə dē) in Blue."

8. **(ret′ər ik)**

   Insincere or exaggerated speech or writing.
   In his campaign (ret′ər ik) the candidate made many empty promises.

9. **(ek′stə sē)**

   Overwhelming joy or delight.
   She was in (ek′stə sē) over winning the beauty contest.

10. **(pal′pə tāt′)**

    To beat rapidly; to throb rapidly.
    You can feel your heart (pal′pə tāt′) when you're excited or afraid.

---

1. wraith
2. apparition
3. cantankerous
4. sublime
5. diarrhea
6. ephemeral
7. rhapsody
8. rhetoric
9. ecstasy
10. palpitate

---

1. **(frən′təs pēs′)**
   An illustration that faces the title page of a book.
   The (frən′təs pēs′) of that dictionary is a portrait
   of Noah Webster.

2. **(fə säd′)**
   a. The front of a building.
   This picture shows the (fə säd′) of a church with
   large white pillars.
   b. A false appearance.
   He put on a (fə säd′) of bravery to hide his
   cowardice.

3. **(im′ə nənt)**
   About to happen; near at hand.
   After the ship struck the iceberg its sinking was
   (im′ə nənt).

4. **(səb sid′ē er ē)**
   A business firm owned by another company.
   That small rubber company is a (səb sid′ē er ē)
   of a large manufacturing corporation.

5. **(kə miz′ə rāt′)**
   To feel sorrow or pity for; to sympathize.
   The defeated champion's friends came to
   (kə miz′ə rāt′) with him.

6. **(bü′mə rang′)**
   A flat curved stick which can be thrown so that it
   returns to the thrower.
   Australian natives can throw a (bü′mə rang′)
   with such accuracy that they use it in hunting.

---

7. **(ə stüt′)** or **(ə styüt′)**
Wise and shrewd; not easily deceived.
He was an (ə stüt′) businessman who made millions of dollars while others lost money.

8. **(sə gā′shəs)**
Wise; shrewd.
The (sə gā′shəs) judge knew right away which of the two men was the real thief.

9. **(är′bə tər)**
Someone chosen to settle differences in a dispute.
Sometimes my father serves as an (är′bə tər) when I argue with my brother.

10. **(tra pēz′)** or **(trə pēz′)**
A swing with a short bar used in acrobatics.
The circus acrobat somersaulted in midair as he swung from one (tra pēz′) to another.

---

1. frontispiece
2. facade
3. imminent
4. subsidiary
5. commiserate
6. boomerang
7. astute
8. sagacious
9. arbiter
10. trapeze

---

1. (biv′wak′) or (biv′ü ak′)
   A temporary camp in the open air.
   While in their (biv′wak′), the soldiers slept under
   pine trees.

2. (biv′wakt′) or (biv′ü akt′)
   Camped temporarily in the open air.
   The soldiers (biv′wakt′) in the valley for the
   night.

3. (kan tōn′mənt) or (kan tän′mənt)
   A group of buildings used for temporary military
   quarters; a large camp for troops.
   Washington's army built many huts as winter
   (kan tōn′mənt) at Valley Forge.

4. (fə nā′gəl)
   To cheat; to get something by trickery.
   He made up all sorts of excuses to (fə nā′gəl)
   his way out of the daily chores.

5. (dif thir′ē ə) or (dip thir′ē ə)
   A serious, contagious disease of the throat.
   The children received immunization injections
   against (dif thir′ē ə).

6. (saf′īr)
   A precious stone of deep blue color.
   The ruby is red; the (saf′īr) is blue.

7. **(rep′lə kə)**

An exact copy.

That model airplane is a miniature (rep′lə kə) of the Wright brothers' first airplane.

8. **(fak sim′ə lē)**

An exact copy.

That book is a (fak sim′ə lē) of the 1843 edition of Dickens's *Christmas Carol*.

9. **(frü ish′ən)**

Fulfillment; realization.

His lifelong dream of becoming a doctor seemed headed for (frü ish′ən) when he graduated from medical school.

10. **(môr′gij)**

A pledge made by a borrower to give up his property if he doesn't pay back money as promised.

The bank holds a (môr′gij) on his house until he pays the money back.

---

1. bivouac
2. bivouacked
3. cantonment
4. finagle
5. diphtheria
6. sapphire
7. replica
8. facsimile
9. fruition
10. mortgage

---

1. **(mā′lā′)** or **(mā lā′)**
   A confused, hand-to-hand fight.
   The demonstrators got into a (mā′lā′) with club-swinging police.

2. **(frā′kəs)**
   A noisy quarrel or fight.
   The (frā′kəs) in the street woke the neighbors.

3. **(kal′əs then′iks)**
   Bodily exercises.
   He did twenty push-ups and twenty knee bends for his morning round of (kal′əs then′iks).

4. **(im′pə təs)**
   A driving force; a forward push.
   His teacher's encouragement was an (im′pə təs) for him to try harder in school.

5. **(prev′ə lənt)**
   Widespread; common.
   That superstition was (prev′ə lənt) among Indians in the West.

6. **(kəl′pə bəl)**
   Deserving blame; guilty.
   The guard who let the prisoner escape was (kəl′pə bəl).

7. **(bləj´ən)**
   A short club with a heavy end.
   The guard beat the prisoners with a (bləj´ən).

8. **(kəj´əl)**
   A short heavy stick.
   The robber hit the man on the head with a
   wooden (kəj´əl).

9. **(fil´ē əl)**
   Befitting a son or a daughter.
   He felt a (fil´ē əl) obligation to care for his
   aged parents.

10. **(äs´ə fī´)**
    To change into bones; to harden.
    The baby's soft skull will (äs´ə fī´) as he grows
    up.

---

1. **melee**
2. **fracas**
3. **calisthenics**
4. **impetus**
5. **prevalent**
6. **culpable**
7. **bludgeon**
8. **cudgel**
9. **filial**
10. **ossify**

---

1. **(i lik′sər)**
   A cure-all; an imaginary liquid believed to cure all diseases or to change common metal into gold.
   He needs an (i lik′sər) that will lift his spirits and free him from boredom.

2. **(al′kə məst)**
   A person who studied medieval chemistry.
   The (al′kə məst) tried to find a method for turning lead into gold.

3. **(pri zəmp′chü əs)**
   Too proud, bold, or daring.
   It was (pri zəmp′chü əs) of the new secretary to ask for a raise after working only a month.

4. **(gab′ər dēn′)**
   A twilled, woven fabric.
   His suit is made of wool (gab′ər dēn′).

5. **(sin′ik)**
   A person who believes that people do things only for selfish reasons.
   The (sin′ik) sneered at anyone who tried to help the poor.

6. **(fə lan′thrə pəst)**
   A person who promotes human welfare by giving generously.
   The great (fə lan′thrə pəst) gave millions of dollars to orphanages and hospitals.

7. **(gùr'mā')** or **(gùr mā')**

A person who loves good food and knows much about it; of or for such a person.

(gùr'mā') cooking is his hobby; he loves to cook fancy dishes for his family and friends.

8. **(es thet'ik)**

Having to do with beauty; artistic.

The architect designed this house for comfort, convenience, and (es thet'ik) appeal.

9. **(kän'ə sər')**

A person who knows enough to act as a critical judge of an art, wine, or food.

They asked the wine (kän'ə sər') which wine to order with the dinner.

10. **(brāl)**

A system of printing for blind people, in which raised dots represent letters, numbers, and punctuation.

A blind person reads (brāl) by feeling dots with his fingertips.

---

1. **elixir**
2. **alchemist**
3. **presumptuous**
4. **gabardine** or **gaberdine**
5. **cynic**
6. **philanthropist**
7. **gourmet**
8. **aesthetic**
9. **connoisseur**
10. **braille**

1. **(par′ə frāz′)**
   To give the meaning of a passage in another form;
   to reword a passage to make it clear.
   "I don't understand these sentences. Please
   (par′ə frāz′) them for me."

2. **(in vā′gəl)** or **(in vē′gəl)**
   To lure by flattery or trickery.
   The boys tried to (in vā′gəl) Jack into paying
   for their movie tickets.

3. **(flú res′ənt)** or **(flô res′ənt)**
   Capable of producing light when exposed to
   radiation or stimulated by electricity.
   The (flú res′ənt) lamp is shaped like a long glass
   tube.

4. **(in′kən des′ənt)**
   Glowing with intense heat.
   The (in′kən des′ənt) lamp Thomas Edison
   invented had a pear-shaped glass bulb.

5. **(kat′ə rakt′)**
   A great downpour; a great, steep waterfall.
   The hurricane brought a (kat′ə rakt′) of rain.

6. **(rē′kə noi′tər)** or **(rek′ə noi′tər)**
   To make a survey; to explore.
   The captain sent a scout to (rē′kə noi′tər) the
   enemy's position.

7. **(ə bis′)**
   A very deep and large hole in the earth; a
   bottomless hole.
   Anyone who slips and falls into that (ə bis′)
   will never get out.

8. **(ə biz′məl)**
   Very deep; hopeless.
   The Great Depression drove many families into
   (ə biz′məl) poverty.

9. **(äl fak′tər ē) or (äl fak′trē)**
   Having the sense of smell.
   The nose is an (äl fak′tər ē) organ.

10. **(däks′hùnt′) or (däks′hùnd′)**
    A small dog with a long body, short legs, and
    drooping ears.
    The (däks′hùnt′) has such short legs that it
    looks like it's crawling when it's running.

---

1. **paraphrase**
2. **inveigle**
3. **fluorescent**
4. **incandescent**
5. **cataract**
6. **reconnoiter**
7. **abyss**
8. **abysmal**
9. **olfactory**
10. **dachshund**

---

1. **(ik skrü′shē ā′ting)** or **(ek skrü′shē ā′ting)**
   Very intense; agonizing.
   When he tried to walk, he felt an
   (ik skrü′shē ā′ting) pain in his injured knee.

2. **(tôr′chǝr ǝs)**
   Causing severe pain; cruelly painful.
   I couldn't bear the dentist's (tôr′chǝr ǝs) drill.

3. **(tôr′chü ǝs)**
   Winding; twisting.
   The road became steep and (tôr′chü ǝs) as we
   drove up the mountainside.

4. **(sin′yü ǝs)**
   Winding; having many curves or turns.
   The snake crawled away, leaving a (sin′yü ǝs)
   trail in the sand.

5. **(kär′bǝ rā′tǝr)** or **(kär′byǝ rā′tǝr)**
   A part of an engine that mixes gasoline with air to
   make it explosive.
   The (kär′bǝ rā′tǝr) has a valve that controls the
   amount of air to be mixed with gasoline.

6. **(sǝp′lǝ kā′shǝn)**
   An earnest and humble request.
   The prisoners fell on their knees and held out
   their hands in (sǝp′lǝ kā′shǝn) for mercy.

7. **(rän′də vü′)** or **(rän′dā vü′)**
A planned meeting; a place for a planned meeting.
During the (rän′də vü′) in space the crews of
the two spaceships visited each other's cabins.

8. **(im′pər tün′)**, **(im′pər tyün′)**, or **(im pôr′chən)**
To ask earnestly, repeatedly, or annoyingly.
Television commercials (im′pər tün′) viewers to
buy many products and services.

9. **(strat′ə jəm)**
A plan or a trick intended to deceive an enemy in
war; a trick; a deception.
The Trojan horse was the Greeks' (strat′ə jəm)
for gaining entrance to Troy.

10. **(är′tə fəs)**
A cunning trick; a clever device.
The Trojan horse was an (är′tə fəs) the Greeks
used to conquer Troy.

---

1. **excruciating**
2. **torturous**
3. **tortuous**
4. **sinuous**
5. **carburetor**
6. **supplication**
7. **rendezvous**
8. **importune**
9. **stratagem**
10. **artifice**

---

1. **(kəm plā′sənt)**
   Pleased with oneself; self-satisfied.
   After winning the earlier games, the players
   became (kəm plā′sənt) and didn't practice hard
   for the championship game.

2. **(kəm plā′sənt) or (kəm plā′zənt)**
   Agreeable and willing to please.
   Our (kəm plā′sənt) coach allowed us to skip
   practice for two days.

3. **(stə kä′tō)**
   Something, as a series of sounds, that is composed
   of or characterized by brief, sharp bursts.
   The loud (stə kä′tō) of automatic gunfire
   shattered the stillness of the night.

4. **(par′ə fər nāl′yə)**
   Equipment; accessories.
   He loaded his car with rods, reel, and other
   fishing (par′ə fər nāl′yə).

5. **(im′pə tənt)**
   Powerless; helpless.
   The team's offense became (im′pə tənt) when the
   quarterback hurt his knee and couldn't play.

6. **(än′trə prə nər′) or (än′trə prə nùr′)**
   A person who takes the risk of starting and
   running a business.
   Henry Ford was a shrewd (än′trə prə nər′) who
   made a great fortune by mass-producing the cars
   he invented.

7. **(bü tēk′)**
   A small store specializing in fashionable clothes and accessories.
   Janet bought her Easter dress at the new (bü tēk′).

8. **(hab′ər dash′ər ē)**
   A store for men's furnishings.
   He bought shirts and ties at the (hab′ər dash′ər ē).

9. **(blas′fə məs)**
   Abusive in speech or writing about God or sacred things.
   The speaker's (blas′fə məs) language angered the pious, churchgoing audience.

10. **(pas′chər ə zā′shən)** or **(pas′tər ə zā′shən)**
    A heating process that destroys harmful germs in milk or other food.
    Before milk is sold, it is heated at a high temperature for (pas′chər ə zā′shən).

---

1. complacent
2. complaisant
3. staccato
4. paraphernalia
5. impotent
6. entrepreneur
7. boutique
8. haberdashery
9. blasphemous
10. pasteurization

1. **(lə krôs′)**
   A ball game played with a long-handled racket.
   The American Indians used animal skulls as balls
   when they played (lə krôs′).

2. **(gäs′ə mər)**
   Light and thin like a cobweb.
   The moon shone through a (gäs′ə mər) cloud.

3. **(fyü′sə läzh′)** or **(fyü′zə läzh′)**
   The main body of an airplane.
   The (fyü′sə läzh′) of that airplane is large
   enough to hold several tanks and trucks.

4. **(fyü′sə läd′)** or **(fyü′sə läd′)**
   A number of shots fired at the same time or
   continuously.
   A (fyü′sə läd′) of machine gun fire rained on the
   enemy.

5. **(bi lē′gərd)**
   Surrounded with troops.
   .The (bi lē′gərd) town asked for food and
   ammunition.

6. **(sed′n ter′ē)**
   Requiring much sitting; sitting much of the time.
   Since he has a (sed′n ter′ē) job at the office, he
   needs a lot of exercise at home.

---

7. **(bůl′yən)**
Gold or silver in bars.
The United States government stores much of its gold (bůl′yən) at Fort Knox, Kentucky.

8. **(bůl′yän)** or **(bůl′yən)**
A clear broth.
I had a cup of chicken (bůl′yän) with my sandwich.

9. **(kän′sə mā′)**
A clear soup made from boiled meat stock.
She boiled chicken for hours, then strained it to make (kän′sə mā′).

10. **(kən səm′ət)** or **(kän′sə mət)**
Excellent; highly skilled; perfect.
That Senator is a (kən səm′ət) politician, who hasn't lost an election in his thirty-year political career.

---

1. lacrosse
2. gossamer
3. fuselage
4. fusillade
5. beleaguered
6. sedentary
7. bullion
8. bouillon
9. consomme
10. consummate

The Final Rounds   *193*

1. **(kas′ə rōl′)**
   A covered baking dish; food baked and served in such a dish.
   She took the shrimp (kas′ə rōl′) out of the oven and served it with rice.

2. **(äb sē′kwē əs)** or **(əb sē′kwē əs)**
   Servile; fawning; overly submissive.
   The bellhop made (äb sē′kwē əs) bows in hope of getting a generous tip.

3. **(sik′ə fənt)**
   One who seeks through flattery to win favor from a person of wealth, power, or influence.
   Like a dog fawning on its master for food, the (sik′ə fənt) praised the king for favors.

4. **(trə vāl′)** or **(trav′āl)**
   Toil; hard labor; painful work.
   It took hardship and (trə vāl′) for the pioneers to live in the wilderness.

5. **(fig′yə rēn′)**
   A small ornamental figure.
   A china (fig′yə rēn′) of a girl stood on the mantel.

6. **(ren′ə säns′)** or **(ren′ə zäns′)**
   A revival; a rebirth.
   A (ren′ə säns′) of interest in tennis spread across the country.

7. **(käm'rad)** or **(käm'rəd)**
   A close friend or companion who works with another for a common purpose.
   The soldiers helped bandage their wounded (käm'rad).

8. **(spän tā'nē əs)**
   Happening naturally and voluntarily.
   When he finished speaking, the crowd burst into (spän tā'nē əs) applause.

9. **(ek stem'pə rā'nē əs)** or **(ik stem'pə rā'nē əs)**
   Performed without preparation.
   He made an (ek stem'pə rā'nē əs) speech thanking the guests for coming to his birthday party.

10. **(im prämp'tü)** or **(im prämp'tyü)**
    Done on the spur of the moment; without previous thought; offhand.
    Mother prepared an (im prämp'tü) lunch for the unexpected guests.

---

1. casserole
2. obsequious
3. sycophant
4. travail
5. figurine
6. renaissance
7. comrade
8. spontaneous
9. extemporaneous
10. impromptu

---

1. **(mīs'trō)**
   A famous conductor, composer, or teacher of
   music; a master in an art.
   The orchestra gave a great performance under the
   direction of the (mīs'trō).

2. **(māl'strəm)**
   A violent whirlpool.
   The canoe was sucked into a (māl'strəm).

3. **(fāt)**
   A gala entertainment; a grand party.
   The ambassador was the guest of honor at the
   garden (fāt).

4. **(ə bliv'ē əs)**
   Not mindful; not aware; not noticing.
   The artist was so busy painting that he was
   (ə bliv'ē əs) of the onlooking crowd.

5. **(tan'tə līz')**
   To tease or torment by holding something desirable
   just out of reach.
   Big apples in tree tops (tan'tə līz') apple pickers
   who can't reach them.

6. **(im pyü'nə tē)**
   Exemption from penalty or punishment.
   Since the ambassador had diplomatic
   (im pyü'nə tē), he didn't have to pay fines for
   parking illegally.

7. **(kä′mə rä′dər ē)**
Goodwill, fellowship, and loyalty among friends or comrades.
Everyone on the team enjoyed the (kä′mə rä′dər ē) of playing football together.

8. **(pres′ə pəs)**
A steep cliff; a steep face of rock.
The mountaineers couldn't climb the (pres′ə pəs) because it was like a wall of ice.

9. **(mem′brän′)**
A thin layer of animal or plant tissue.
The egg shell and the (mem′brän′) protect the white and the yolk.

10. **(dī′ə fram′)**
A wall of muscle that separates the chest from the abdomen.
These breathing exercises will strengthen your (dī′ə fram′) and help improve your voice.

---

1. maestro
2. maelstrom
3. fete
4. oblivious
5. tantalize
6. impunity
7. camaraderie
8. precipice
9. membrane
10. diaphragm

---

1. **(as′ə nĭn′)**
   Very stupid or silly.
   We were embarrassed by his (as′ə nĭn′) remarks.

2. **(äb tüs′), (äb tyüs′), (əb tüs′),** or **(əb tyüs′)**
   Slow to understand; not sensitive; dull.
   He was too (äb tüs′) to see that the joke was on him.

3. **(lab′ə rĭnth′)**
   A maze; a place full of confusing passages.
   They became lost in the (lab′ə rĭnth′) of the cave.

4. **(pri kō′shəs)**
   Showing skills or maturity earlier than usual.
   The (pri kō′shəs) child began reading newspapers when he was three years old.

5. **(mär′tər dəm)**
   The suffering of torture or death rather than giving up one's beliefs or principles.
   The saint would rather die in (mär′tər dəm) than live in shame.

6. **(əl′tə mā′təm)** or **(əl′tə mä′təm)**
   A final demand or condition offered by one of the parties in negotiation.
   "Surrender by midnight, or we will attack" was the general's (əl′tə mā′təm).

7. **(krev′əs)**
   A narrow crack or split.
   A rattlesnake crawled out of a (krev′əs) in the rock.

8. **(krə vas′)** or **(kri vas′)**
   A deep crack, as in a glacier, a dam, or an embankment.
   The (krə vas′) in the glacier was too wide for them to cross.

9. **(del′i kə tes′ən)**
   A store that sells ready-to-eat food.
   She bought chicken salad and pickles at the (del′i kə tes′ən).

10. **(mez′ə nēn′)** or **(mez′ə nēn′)**
    A half story or a balcony between two stories of a building.
    We went up to the (mez′ə nēn′) and looked down on the first floor.

---

1. **asinine**
2. **obtuse**
3. **labyrinth**
4. **precocious**
5. **martyrdom**
6. **ultimatum**
7. **crevice**
8. **crevasse**
9. **delicatessen**
10. **mezzanine**

---

1. **(gran′jər)** or **(gran′jür)**
   Greatness; splendor.
   "When we saw the Grand Canyon, we marveled at its (gran′jər)."

2. **(sim′ə trē)**
   A balanced arrangement of parts on the two sides of a center line.
   A snowflake has beautiful (sim′ə trē).

3. **(kav′əl kād′)** or **(kav′əl kād′)**
   A procession of horsemen or carriages.
   A (kav′əl kād′) of mounted police led the parade.

4. **(kən fet′ē)**
   Small pieces of colored paper thrown about in celebration.
   (kən fet′ē) streamed from office windows, welcoming the hero's motorcade.

5. **(yü′kə lā′lē)**
   A small four-stringed musical instrument resembling a guitar.
   Todd strummed his (yü′kə lā′lē) and sang a Hawaiian dance song.

6. **(fə nal′ē)** or **(fə nä′lē)**
   The last part of a performance; the end.
   They sang a joyful chorus during the opera's (fə nal′ē).

7. **(shan'də lir')**
   A hanging light fixture with branches holding light
   bulbs or candles.
   A crystal (shan'də lir') hangs from a high
   ceiling of the dining room.

8. **(kan'dl ä'brəm)** or **(kan'dl ā'brəm)**
   A decorative candlestick with several branches.
   Diane lighted all six candles on the silver
   (kan'dl ä'brəm).

9. **(mar'ē ə net')**
   A puppet with jointed limbs made to move by
   strings from above.
   Laura pulled the strings up and down to make
   the (mar'ē ə net') dance.

10. **(ven tril'ə kwəst)**
    A person skilled in speaking so that his or her
    voice seems to come from another person or from
    a puppet.
    John, a (ven tril'ə kwəst), spoke for the toy
    soldier at the puppet show.

---

1. **grandeur**
2. **symmetry**
3. **cavalcade**
4. **confetti**
5. **ukulele**
6. **finale**
7. **chandelier**
8. **candelabrum**
9. **marionette**
10. **ventriloquist**

The Final Rounds   *201*

Spelling Bees in These United States

What are spelling bees like?
How can you succeed in them?

Here are some informative scenes and helpful hints.

Riverside, California (Press-Enterprise)
Copyright © 1982, Press-Enterprise, reprinted with permission

"When's lunch?"

That's what David Edwards said right after he won the Riverside County Spelling Bee.

Matching wits with 24 other school district champion spellers at Raincross Square yesterday worked up his appetite. It also won him a trip to Washington, D.C., May 31 through June 4, to compete in the national contest.

By the time David reached the final word, "triage," he had spelled 29 other words correctly. "I knew 'triage' because I saw it at a hospital once," he said.

During the last five rounds, David kept the officials running to the dictionary when he asked for the definition and any other correct pronounciations of words (according to Webster) before attempting to spell.

It paid off.

He could have tripped up on the second-to-last word "rheumy" (pronounced roomy) had he not asked what it meant. Howard Fisher, the spelling master, explained that "rheumy" means discharging, such as during an eye infection.

"You mean 'rheum' is the discharge and your eyes are giving the discharge?" David asked Fisher.

Yep. So the seventh grader from Alessandro Junior High in Sunnymead took a stab at it and got it right.

"Triage" and "rheumy" weren't the toughest words he spelled though. Earlier, the audience made a stir when he spelled "ptarmigan" quickly and without faltering.

When the contest was over, David stood in front of the stage accepting congratulatory handshakes from everyone who walked by. His mother, Norma, had tears welling up in her eyes when she ran up to give him a hug. "And his mother is a housewife who can't spell," she said.

His father, Leonard, a steelworker at Kaiser Steel's Fontana Plant, beamed with pride, as did David's adult brother, Larry, who is also employed by Kaiser.

During the contest it was easy to spot relatives and teachers of each speller. Every time it was a student's turn to spell, a different cluster of people in the audience sat holding their breath and clenching their fists. When the turn was over, they slumped in their chairs while the tension shifted to another speller's parents.

Louisville, Kentucky (The Courier-Journal)

Copyright © 1980, The Courier-Journal, reprinted with permission

The fourth- through eighth-graders displayed surprising cool as they stepped up to the microphone in the contest room at the Commonwealth Convention Center in Louisville.

The most visible display of nerves occurred when moderator Betty Mainord of The Courier-Journal and The Louisville Times suggested that everyone take a deep breath before the start. A ripple of relief bobbed across the rows of students.

The youngest contestant, Barren County fourth-grader Vivian Bruner, heaved a sigh of relief and a big smile spread across her face as she sounded out the word "binoculars" and spelled it correctly.

Spellers' styles varied from the nerveless to the nervous. Twiddling thumbs, clasped hands, sudden slips on simple words showed that the outer calm was sometimes a facade.

Eleven-year-old Steven Lakes from Madison County was the first speller eliminated when he was asked to spell "squat."

"S—k," he said and the truth bell clanged him out.

"I don't know what made me think s—k," he said later. He was a Madison County winner last year but fell by the wayside in the state contest when he couldn't spell "jubilant."

Fingers snapped when a slip of the tongue caused another speller to begin "chef" with an s—h instead of a c—h, and another started "growl" with a g—r—a.

Some of the spellers adopted a sing-song style, pairing letters to be sure to get them all in.

Others used a rat-a-tat-tat style. Jason Kissner, a fifth-grader from Oldham County, seemed to be staring at each letter written on an invisible blackboard when he carefully spelled out p—e—r—s—u—a—s—i—v—e.

The rules called for each student to pronounce the word before spelling it to verify that the contestant understood the word. The wisdom of that practice was evident when one student during a practice run didn't understand the request to spell "eye" until it was pronounced "ahye."

One boy may have wished he had repeated the word he was asked to spell before he plunged ahead. He spelled "set" when he was asked to spell "sect."

When in doubt, many spellers showed how much they had learned about the tricks of the English language as they guessed at words and chose a harder way to spell them. One girl unfamiliar with the word "infamous" took a sophisticated stab at it: i—n—p—h—a . . .

Kenneth, who spelled "numen" and the last word needed to wrap up his victory, "emollient," won a trip to the National Spelling Bee in Washington, D.C. He will also receive a set of the Encyclopedia Britannica.

For second place, Andrea won a $200 U.S. Savings Bond and an American Heritage Dictionary.

Marcella won a $100 U.S. Savings Bond and The World Almanac for third place.

All of the contestants received trophies.

Miami, Florida (The Miami Herald)

By 3:30 p.m. Thursday, the 198 good spellers had been boiled down to two great spellers of very different styles.

Mara Shlackman, a sixth grader at Neva King Cooper Elementary, is a slow, slow speller. Even the easy words in the early rounds—like "prescription," she spelled very slowly. The betting among those who knew spelling at the Barry College Auditorium was [that] Mara Shlackman, No. 21—one of the smallest and youngest contestants—would be blown away early on.

A bad bet.

Javier Tam, on the other hand, a tall, mature eighth grader from John F. Kennedy Junior High, is a lightning-quick speller. He spelled out "quadragenarian," faster than most people can say "40."

For 10 minutes Lightning Javier Tam and Tiny Mara Shlackman slugged it out, word for word.

"P-a-g-i-n-a-t-i-o-n," spelled Tiny Mara.

"L-o-g-i-s-t-i-c-i-a-n," countered Lightning Javier.

"H-e-m-o-p-h-i-l-i-a," spelled Mara.

"D-e-m-i-t-a-s-s-e," countered Lightning.

"S-c-h-e-r-z-o," sang Mara.

"B-a-n-a-l-i-t-y," replied Javier.

It seemed like they would go on deep into the night. Mara and Javier, Javier and Mara, spelling anything that got in their way.

Until that "scampi."

"Scampi" of all things! A shrimp of a word. Mara spelled "xystus," without blinking. "Scampi" would be a piece of cake, everyone figured.

A bad bet.

Mara slipped on the scampi: "S-c-a-m-p-y."

The judges rang the bell.

Javier scampered to the microphone and spelled it right on the nose. He clinched his victory with "dachshund."

No, it hadn't been easy, but Javier Tam was the 36th Miami Herald Dade County Spelling Bee champ.

He had started Thursday morning with 197 other Dade elementary and junior high students, all champions at their public or private schools.

Part one was a written test, 50 words' worth.

The twenty-seven who had 17 or less mistakes made it to the final, oral round.

Good spellers, like David Centner of Rockway Junior High. "I'm a natural speller," explained David. David's grandfather and grandmother Irving and Anne Loeb were there, along with his sister Helen, his Mom Sylvia and Dad Herman, a doctor. Many Centners have been great, proud spellers.

The 27 finalists sat on the Barry College stage, listening to their final briefing. "OK, happy spellers, are you ready?" asked Al Dilthey, community relations director of The Herald.

The happy spellers barely shook their heads "Yes." Obviously, they were saving their energy for big words.

Dilthey explained that if a contestant spelled a word wrong, the judges would ring a bell, and the contestant was supposed to leave.

"The bell will ring," he said, "and you can come back next year."

Jose Talleda fiddled with the number around his neck. Scott Turner blew his nose. Kathryn Clark stared blankly at the large audience. Even good spellers get a little uneasy at the thought of "The Bell."

"If you hear the bell," said Dilthey, "walk off stage right and that charming lady will shake your hand and give you a dictionary."

Everyone stared straight ahead. That was one charming lady nobody wanted to meet.

For the first few rounds, nobody went out. Then the words got tougher, and the bell rang. Pretty soon, it sounded like there was an elevator arriving every minute.

Linda Akers of Centennial Junior High went down on "dogdom." "In all of dogdom," the pronouncer said, "Lassie was unique. Dogdom."

"D-o-g-d-u-m," Linda said.

After she met the charming lady, Linda was asked how she made the mistake.

"I just didn't know how to spell it," she said. Not an uncommon explanation.

Washington, D.C. (Rocky Mountain News, Denver, Colorado)

Copyright © 1982, Rocky Mountain News, reprinted with permission

WASHINGTON—How does someone go about winning a national spelling bee? Florence Bailly should know.

She is the mother of Jacques Bailly, who won the bee in 1980. She also is the coach for Molly Dieveney, who Thursday won the 1982 National Spelling Bee in Washington.

First, she suggests using the "Words of the Champions," which is published each year and provided by newspapers that sponsor the bees in their areas.

Bailly saves back copies of the book, which is the bible for most spellers in the national bee.

In addition, Bailly compiles lists of words used at bees around the country, including the national ones held each year in Washington.

Then she emphasizes learning the roots of the words on the lists. With Molly, she says, "I started out with telephone.

"I said, 'Molly, do you know how to spell telephone?'

"She spelled it correctly. Then I said, 'Do you know what it means?'

"She said the usual—the thing that hangs on the wall.

"Do you know it is comprised of two Greek words, 'tele,' meaning distance, and 'phone,' meaning sound?

"She looked at me and said, 'Does that mean it is the same for television and telegraph?'

"She connected it that fast—without any coaching—and that's when I knew," Bailly said.

With Molly, Bailly started with the 1980 "Words of the Champions" and then moved on to the 1981 version when that was available.

They began right after Jacques won the Colorado-Wyoming Bee in 1980 and studied non-stop until Thursday.

"I gave her a 1980 book and wrote in it 'To a future spelling bee champion.'

"She has studied in a systematic way from the beginning.

"I will analyze this year's Washington list," Bailly said. "One of the biggest helps with Jacques was Mrs. Kerwin (mother of 1979 national champ Katie Kerwin) who offered me Katie's list."

"Underneath it all." Bailly said, "It's still a competition. The spelling bee is the goal, the coach is the catalyst and the child and parents have to do the work."

"I became convinced the spelling bee was a worthwhile thing if it is approached right. Don't turn the kids into parrots—teach them roots. There is no way to fake it."

Index

complacent, 191
complaisant, 191
comrade, 195
concerto, 87
conciliatory, 171
concoction, 89
condescend, 165
condolence, 113
condominium, 141
confetti, 201

congeal, 57
congenital, 121
conglomerate, 151
connoisseur, 185
connotation, 45
consecrate, 147
consomme, 193
consummate, 193
contentious, 111
conundrum, 37

convalesce, 15
conversant, 103
convivial, 59
copious, 31
coroner, 83
correlation, 107
corroborate, 131
corrugated, 57
corsage, 37
countenance, 107

coup, 5
coupe, 5
courier, 49
covenant, 35
coyote, 23
cravat, 19
credence, 53
credulous, 53

crescendo, 3
crevasse, 199
crevice, 199
criterion, 19
critique, 21
crochet, 5
croquet, 3
crystalline, 117
crystallize, 117
cudgel, 183

cuisine, 137
culinary, 137
culmination, 69
culpable, 183
currant, 17
cursory, 139
cutlery, 27
cynic, 185

D

dachshund, 187
dahlia, 53
dalmatian, 161
deacon, 125
debacle, 145
debut, 95
declivity, 97
decorum, 111
decrepit, 113
deign, 165

delicatessen, 199
demeanor, 93
demur, 83
demure, 83
dereliction, 163
derogatory, 119
despicable, 105
destitute, 175

desultory, 173
deterioration, 47
deterrent, 93
detrimental, 117
dextrous, 143
diabetes, 147
diabolic, 101
diacritical, 83
diaphragm, 197
diarrhea, 177

diesel, 9
diffident, 155
diffusion, 15
dilapidated, 113
dilemma, 11
diminutive, 77
dinghy, 125
diocese, 17
diphtheria, 181
dirge, 67

dirigible, 65
disburse, 99
discomfiture, 55
discordant, 25
discreet, 65
discretion, 65
dissertation, 33
dissident, 75
dissipate, 41
dissonant, 25

distaff, 55
distraught, 41
divers, 45
diverse, 45
divot, 49
dowager, 43
duress, 73

E

eccentric, 17
ecstasy, 177
eddy, 49
edifice, 143
edify, 169
efficacious, 159
effigy, 113
effrontery, 155
elegy, 97
elicit, 29

elite, 133
elixir, 185
ellipse, 101
emaciated, 77
emancipation, 93
embezzlement, 85
embryo, 105
emerald, 27
empirical, 135
enamel, 23

encompass, 19
encumbrance, 87
enervating, 59
enigma, 37
ennoble, 107
ensconce, 135
ensemble, 149
entourage, 175
entree, 3
entrepreneur, 191

enunciation, 21
ephemeral, 177
epilogue, 173
epitaph, 173
epitome, 173
equinox, 9

equivocate, 167
escapade, 125
etymology, 113
eulogize, 51
euphemism, 51
euphonious, 51
exalt, 71
exasperation, 89
excruciating, 189
exhilarating, 109

exhort, 71
exigency, 111
exodus, 165
exorbitant, 127
expedient, 57
expedite, 57
expeditious, 57
expertise, 105
explicit, 173
extemporaneous, 195

extol, 51
extraneous, 121
extravagance, 97
extricate, 11
exuberant, 69
exude, 87
exult, 71
exultant, 71

F

fabricate, 51
facade, 179
facetious, 77
facile, 79
facsimile, 181
fallacious, 87
fallacy, 87
farce, 133

feasible, 79
felony, 93
fervor, 85
festal, 55
fete, 197
fetish, 81
feudal, 107
fiasco, 145
fiendish, 101
figurine, 195

filial, 183
finagle, 181
finale, 201
finesse, 165
firmament, 167
fjord, 15
flaccid, 117
flagrant, 121
flamboyant, 129
flamingo, 143

flippantly, 141
florid, 7
flotilla, 11
flotsam, 71
fluorescent, 187
foray, 73
forte, 109
fracas, 183
fraudulent, 85
frenetic, 113

freshet, 167
frivolous, 141
frontispiece, 179
fruition, 181
fuselage, 193
fusillade, 193

N

nadir, 137
naive, 7
nicotine, 39
niggardly, 95
nightingale, 31
nocturnal, 137
nominal, 109
nonchalance, 141
noxious, 117

O

obeisance, 143
obelisk, 45
oblique, 175
obliterate, 51
oblivious, 197
obnoxious, 117
obsequious, 195
obsession, 81
obtuse, 199
occult, 169

odious, 103
ogre, 131
olfactory, 187
omnipotent, 43
omniscient, 43
omnivorous, 43
opaque, 151
opportune, 57
oracle, 37
orchid, 35

ordinance, 139
ordnance, 139
oriole, 31
orthodontist, 85
orthodox, 85

oscillation, 155
ossify, 183
ostentatious, 151
ottoman, 77

P

palatable, 67
palate, 67
palatial, 135
palette, 67
pallet, 67
palpitate, 177
paltry, 47
panorama, 5
paradox, 35
paramount, 79

paraphernalia, 191
paraphrase, 187
parlance, 97
parlay, 169
parley, 169
parody, 133
pasteurization, 191
pathos, 159
patriarch, 135
pediatrician, 23

pellet, 67
penitence, 81
penitentiary, 81
perceptible, 73
perennial, 115
perimeter, 31
periscope, 31
perjury, 27
permeate, 23
pernicious, 159
peruse, 13
petite, 9

petrify, 49
petulant, 119
petunia, 5
pewter, 25
pharaoh, 169
philanthropist, 185
physicist, 109
physique, 103
piccolo, 93
picturesque, 87

piedmont, 57
pillage, 77
piquant, 107
pique, 19
pittance, 47
placate, 157
plagiarism, 137
planetarium, 29
platinum, 33
plausible, 79

plummet, 5
pneumatic, 91
poignant, 115
poinsettia, 121
polyglot, 27
porcelain, 23
porridge, 45
posse, 13
prate, 37
precarious, 165

precipice, 197
precocious, 199
preliminary, 47
premier, 3
premiere, 3
presumptuous, 185
pretzel, 79
prevalent, 183

primeval, 175
prodigal, 129
prodigy, 23
profiteering, 119
prolific, 121
promissory, 133
propitious, 129
prosaic, 149
pseudonym, 17
psychiatrist, 41

psychology, 41
pugilist, 41
pugnacious, 111
pungent, 107
purgatory, 127
purl, 137
putrefy, 49
putrid, 49

Q

quadruple, 9
quagmire, 41
quandary, 11
quarantine, 37
quartz, 81
quay, 15
querulous, 119
queue, 171
quizzical, 63

R

ramshackle, 63
rancor, 89
ravenous, 91
reciprocate, 99
recluse, 87
recompense, 99
reconciliation, 171

reconnoiter, 187
recoup, 15
recuperate, 15
redundant, 173
regale, 69
regime, 67
rehabilitation, 95
reimburse, 99
reiterate, 115
relegate, 145

reminisce, 15
reminiscent, 15
renaissance, 195
rendezvous, 189
renegade, 157
renege, 157
repertoire, 163
replete, 55
replica, 181
requisite, 143

rescind, 175
residue, 101
respite, 99
resplendent, 151
resurrection, 125
resuscitate, 101
retaliate, 25
reticent, 61
retinue, 175
reveille, 171

revelry, 65
reverberate, 103
reverie, 173
rhapsody, 177
rhetoric, 177
rheumatism, 141
rhinoceros, 151
rhubarb, 105

ricochet, 5
rivulet, 67
rosette, 55
rotund, 57
rudimentary, 85
ruffian, 143
ruminant, 63
russet, 97

S

Sabbath, 107
sabotage, 161
sacrament, 165
safari, 11
sagacious, 179
sapphire, 181
sarcasm, 131
sardonic, 131
satiated, 91
satire, 133

saute, 61
scabbard, 89
scaffold, 29
scalpel, 3
scenario, 109
scepter, 29
scourge, 121
scrupple, 139
scrupulous, 139
scrutiny, 47

scullery, 111
secede, 23
secession, 23
sedentary, 193
seditious, 101
seismograph, 87
semaphore, 89
seminar, 25

seminary, 25
serenade, 141
settee, 17
shellac, 35
sierra, 43
silhouette, 101
simile, 161
simultaneous, 135
sinewy, 91
sinuous, 189

skeptical, 53
skewer, 65
skirmish, 59
sleazy, 33
snobbery, 47
snorkel, 111
sobriety, 33
sodden, 153
sojourn, 19
solace, 113

solder, 31
solicit, 69
solicitous, 69
soliloquy, 71
solitaire, 71
solstice, 9
sombrero, 23
sonorous, 157
sophisticated, 7
sorcerer, 159

sordid, 83
sorority, 39
sorrel, 49
specious, 169
spontaneous, 195
sporadic, 79
squalid, 83
squalor, 83

staccato, 191
stalwart, 147
stamina, 3
stethoscope, 145
stirrup, 69
stoic, 161
stolid, 161
stratagem, 189
stupefied, 123
stupor, 123

suave, 149
sublime, 177
subsidiary, 179
subterranean, 123
succinct, 63
succor, 113
succumb, 39
suffrage, 97
sumptuous, 99
supercilious, 139

supersede, 163
supplication, 189
surfeit, 91
surveillance, 117
susceptible, 99
sustenance, 113
sycophant, 195
symmetry, 201
synthesis, 63
syringe, 85

T

tacit, 61
taciturn, 61
talisman, 81
tambourine, 37
tangible, 73
tantalize, 197

tassel, 83
tawny, 77
temerity, 155
temperance, 33
tenacious, 73
tendrils, 53
tenuous, 51
terminology, 47
terrain, 123
terrestrial, 123

terse, 63
tetanus, 47
therapeutic, 137
thesaurus, 9
thrall, 147
throes, 105
tiara, 63
tirade, 137
titular, 155
torpid, 59

torpor, 59
torrential, 13
tortuous, 189
torturous, 189
tourniquet, 49
trampoline, 29
trapeze, 179
travail, 195
trellis, 39
trepidation, 73

troupe, 71
tubercular, 127
tuberculosis, 127
tumultuous, 45
turbid, 151
turgid, 151
turquoise, 47
tutelage, 83

Words I want to remember

Words I want to remember

_____

_____

_____

_____

_____

_____

_____

_____

_____

_____

_____

_____

_____

_____

_____

_____

I would like to order *THE SPELLING BEE SPELLER:*

In Paperback Edition

____ copies of Volume 1, THE FIRST ROUND, paperback $7.95 each

____ copies of Volume 2, THE MIDDLE ROUNDS, paperback $7.95 each

____ copies of Volume 3, THE FINAL ROUNDS, paperback $7.95 each

____ sets of Volume 1, 2 & 3 listed above, paperback $19.85 each
(a savings of $4.00 a set)

Please add $2.00 to cover postage and handling.

Amount enclosed $_____

Name _____

Address _____

City _____

State _____ Zip _____

Mail this page along with your check or money order to:

Hondale Inc.
553 Auburndale Avenue
Akron, Ohio 44313

Cut along this line and mail

Have you interesting stories about spelling bees you have participated in? Please share your stories with us.

Have you any suggestions for improving *THE SPELLING BEE SPELLER*? We welcome your ideas.

Please send your stories or suggestions to:

Editor, The Spelling Bee Speller
Hondale, Inc.
553 Auburndale Avenue
Akron, Ohio 44313

If your stories or suggestions are used in forthcoming series of *The Spelling Bee Speller*, we will notify you and send you a special gift.

If you need additional plastic SPELLMARKs, please send 50 cents for each one and a self-addressed stamped envelope to Hondale, Inc., 553 Auburndale Avenue, Akron, Ohio 44313.